The Illustrated Book of Wargrave

Sunlit Backwater (Wargrave)

The Illustrated
Book of Wargrave

Edited by

Peter Halman and Peter Delaney

Wargrave Local History Society

Copyright © 2011 Wargrave Local History Society

Published by Wargrave Local History Society, Wargrave, Berkshire

Printed and bound by CPI Antony Rowe, Bumper's Farm, Chippenham, Wiltshire

ISBN   978 0 9511878 5 2

Copyright of the photographs and illustrations belongs to those credited in the list of contributors on page 100.

We wish to acknowledge all who have helped with this book, but if, inadvertently, we have omitted to credit the owner of the copyright in any image, the Wargrave Local History Society would be pleased to make a correction in any future edition of this book.

The front cover illustration shows sheep-dipping in the River Thames at The St George & Dragon in 1897.

The back cover illustration shows Mill Green at Wargrave.

Foreword

Wargrave is an active parish and the Wargrave Local History Society plays a full part. Led by their officers and committee there is a monthly programme of talks and visits. Formed in 1981 the Society has produced two Books of Wargrave written predominantly by local people. They have been a great success.

This is now the third book of Wargrave but of a different character to its predecessors. This time advantage has been taken of a steadily increasing archive of photographs and other documentation, largely introduced by caring donors. This is fascinating material and gives an important interpretation of the growth of the village over past periods.

An area wider than the village has experienced dramatic growth caused at least in part by the excellent communications with the rest of the country and general growth in the UK economy particularly in the South East. This has been paralleled by a concentration of services into larger towns. You will see within these pages a much altered High Street and an inference that Wargrave was guided by relatively few individuals from the larger houses. The present position is different with a far larger number of people with varied experience influencing constructively and positively the character of the village. Whilst some may regret the changes from the old Wargrave, and indeed some are regrettable, the village has kept a splendid character due to the efforts of the villagers.

Wargrave has been well served by the members of this Society, all volunteers, who have participated in the creation of this book right up to the production stage.

I commend this book to Wargrave villagers, visitors and anyone interested in the development of a character created by those who have lived there.

Remnant

President
Wargrave Local History Society
April 2011

A Brief History of Wargrave

There has been a village at Wargrave for a very long time. The earliest documentary evidence for the village is a charter dated 1061, whilst the Domesday survey, completed in 1086 refers to Wargrave, with the Manor of Wargrave belonging to the King. This states that before 1066 it had belonged to Queen Edith, the wife of Edward the Confessor. What is apparent is that the village was already well established by that time. The survey records that Wargrave's 5000 acres were populated by around 250 people. The village was valued at £27/6/8d - one of the richest, and most populous, places in East Berkshire. There were weirs on the river - which had eel traps that produced 3000 eels per year - and this area was surrounded by groves (areas of woodland) of the Windsor Forest, which at the time stretched as far as the River Thames at Wargrave. This gives the most likely explanation for how the village gained its name (which is written Weregreave on early documents) - a grove by a weir. Wheat, barley, oats, corn and peas formed the main crops, whilst sheep, pigs, and poultry were among the livestock. By 1300, the population had risen to about 3-400, despite famines in 1257/8 and 1270/72.

In the early medieval period, most of the houses were on Mill Green, close to the church. They were built of locally available, but not long lasting, materials and so needed frequent repair to the timber, thatch etc., creating work for the local craftsmen who were an essential part of village life; carpenters, masons, wheelwrights, coopers, tanners, potters, blacksmiths, bakers, millers, ploughmen, carters and shepherds all providing specialist skills for the villagers. However, the population of Wargrave fell in the mid-fourteenth century, due to the Black Death. Wargrave was relatively poor by 1340 - about 10% of the population died annually from starvation - and the weakened population could not cope with the arrival of the bubonic plague. Within Berkshire, only Wargrave appears to have been savagely hit in both the plagues of 1349 and 1361. Due to the loss of manpower, no threshing or hurdle-making was done - threshing was a communal activity, but there was no 'community' there. A series of dry summers and bumper crops in the 1370s and 1390s brought renewed prosperity to Wargrave, however, and life began to return to normal.

Burning the infected properties was one way to eradicate the plague, and this was apparently the method used in Wargrave. Timber Cottage - believed to be the oldest surviving cottage in the village - was built mid-fourteenth century. Other timber buildings appeared in the High Street in the early fifteenth century, including The Bull, strategically located at the crossroads. The village centre therefore moved from Mill Green to the High Street. Most of the farmhouses were also found there - Hamilton House (High Street) and Ouseleys (School Lane) still remaining. The fields around the village were largely farmed on the strip system. Tithes had to be paid and in 1634 were levied on wood for poles, faggots and walking sticks, osiers, grass on eyots, lambs, calves, colts, pigs, cygnets, honey, wax, ale, pigeons, soft fruit and poultry (geese and turkeys). Tithes were also payable on garden produce, including roots, seeds, onions, garlic, flax and hemp, apples and pears. The woodland was of major value, providing timber for making furniture and farm and domestic tools and utensils.

The church at Wargrave is first mentioned in a charter dated 1121, when Henry I gave it to Reading Abbey. Soon after, a stone structure was erected, and the oldest part of the present building - the north wall - is probably part of that early church. The present tower dates from 1635 and is an inner tower of chalk, with a brick outer. The main structure of the church, however, dates from after the 1914 fire - discovered in the early hours of Whit-Monday that year. It was strongly rumoured, although not proven, that the fire was caused by suffragettes - the Diocesan architect's report says the fire had begun in several places in the church. The fire was so fierce that all the timber was destroyed, and much of the stonework made unsafe by the heat, so that the aisle pillars and south wall had to be replaced. The new roof beams are of larger section than might be expected, in order to brace the retained north wall. The tower acted like a chimney, and the timber, clock and the six bells dating from 1668-88 were all destroyed. The rebuilt church was consecrated on July 22nd 1916 - the opportunity being taken to extend the church by one bay at the eastern end. The fire also destroyed many memorials and the stained glass windows. Fortunately, the church registers - from 1538, the brass altar cross - dated June 1887 and the church plate - including an Elizabethan chalice and paten all survived, as did the large brass eagle lectern - its base is engraved 'This lectern was saved from the fire which destroyed the Church June 1st 1914' - it is reported that it took four men to lift it.

The district was essentially agricultural, and many of the farming families remained here for long periods - names such as A'Bear for example being recorded from 1340 until 1925. However, change was starting to occur, and by the late eighteenth century, and again through the Victorian and Edwardian era, Wargrave became a fashionable place by the river, for those who loved to paint, and those who wanted to go boating or fishing. Large houses appeared along the river frontage, and more humble dwellings were built for the farm workers as the village expanded. The village schools - at that stage in the High Street - were founded by Robert Piggott by 1796. Meanwhile, a workhouse had been set up on the (then) edge of the village in the 1770s in what is now Victoria Road. Other parts of the parish, such as Crazies Hill and Cockpole Green remained rural, whilst Hare Hatch and Kiln Green served the needs of travellers in the carriages and stage coaches on the Bath Road. Large mansions were erected in this part of the parish - within easy reach of the main road, but largely out of sound and sight of it. As the 19th century progressed, so the village expanded further - principally along Victoria Road. A new school building was erected on School Hill in 1862 to cater for the growing population, whilst the previous year, a school had been erected at Crazies Hill - in both cases paid for by subscriptions from the local inhabitants.

Although the railway had opened to Twyford in 1841, Wargrave was not provided with a station until 1900. This made it easier for those who worked in London to live in the village, and so some further building took place to provide for these early 'commuters' - such as the larger houses of Braybrooke Road. In essence, however, Wargrave remained a largely rural place. It was in the early 1900s that Mrs Smith provided the village with many of the amenities that it now enjoys - the Almshouses, Woodclyffe Hall, Woodclyffe Hostel, allot-ments and recreation ground with its Pavilion (Woodclyffe being the name of her house on the Henley Road). It was during this period that houseboats first became popular - notably along the River Loddon - many to later be hauled onto the bank and be developed into more permanent homes.

The effect of the First World War was to take many of the men away to join the services - well over 50 never to return. Otherwise, life for the residents continued much the same as before, although the Woodclyffe Hall and Hostel were used as a hospital for wounded soldiers. The Second World War, however, saw the establishment of an American army base on land at the top of Victoria Road, and a number of other sites were requisitioned for use in connection with the war effort, such as Hennerton House, or an area off Tag Lane, which became a prisoner of war camp. Many families took in children who had been evacuated to avoid the effects of the bombing on London. The children attended the local schools - including the new Piggott School for the older pupils that had opened in 1940. Fortunately, no-one was injured by any of the few bombs that fell on the parish of Wargrave.

After the war, there was a desperate need for more housing. The army base had been vacated, but the concrete road on the site made it difficult to return the land to agriculture, and so the houses were built that now form Highfield Park. Further house building took place during the 1950s and 1960s - some as 'infill' between the existing houses of Victoria Road, or to develop Station Road, or other areas of land, such as Watermans Way (on part of the boatyard site). The largest development was that which gradually took over the former Fidlers Farm, to create Purfield Drive, Langhams Way, Ridgeway, and the roads adjoining them - providing for a further 250 families. The largest proportion of the village population, therefore, no longer lived close to the High Street core, and this led to the move of the surgery to Victoria Road in 1975, soon followed by the chemist's, whilst most of the High Street shops that had provided for the 'everyday' needs of the village no longer did so.

Wargrave has changed from being a predominantly agricultural village to one which is now, largely, seen as a residential area for those who work elsewhere, with the 2001 census recording the population of the parish of Wargrave as having grown to 3910. Despite this, however, it retains an essentially village feel to it - one that has a wide range of societies and activities to cater for young and old, arranges a biennial village festival for the community as a whole, and an 'atmosphere' that encourages people to return.

Peter Delaney

The Illustrated
Book of Wargrave

Historical Images of a Berkshire Village

Editors' note

The majority of the images in this book are from the Wargrave Local History Society's archives but several were kindly loaned by villagers or others with a family connection. Their names appear in the Acknowledgments section and we thank them most warmly for their generous support. The book's contents reflect the material available to us rather than presenting a comprehensive and balanced account of village history, such as can be found in *The Book of Wargrave* and *The Second Book of Wargrave* published by the Society.

A large number of the images are from postcards, many of them more than a hundred years old. Inevitably, some have been damaged or marked and we have made careful and sympathetic use of computer software to restore them to a little nearer their original condition. No material changes have been made and we would be happy to open our archives to any reader who wishes to inspect the original prints.

Bird's-eye view 1

St Mary's Church and Wargrave Court are in the bottom right-hand corner and Wargrave Manor is in the top left-hand corner. The straight line of the cottages in School Lane can be seen at the top right, leading up to Victoria Road. The Chiltern Towers Hotel, later known as Hill Lands, is in the centre background. To the left of that is a walled garden belonging to the Manor and the large greenhouses further to the left stand in what is now The Vinery on Wargrave Hill. The photograph was taken in the early 1920s.

Bird's-eye view 2

The central part of the village had not changed greatly during the forty years prior to 1965 when this photograph was taken. The only significant number of new houses had been built at Highfield Park, on the site of the former American army camp. Now, however, substantial private housing development was taking place.

This view shows The St George & Dragon on the left-hand edge, Highfield Park at the centre of the top edge and Wargrave Court on Mill Green in the bottom right-hand corner. Church Street and School Lane run up the right-hand side, leading to Victoria Road. In the centre of the picture the new blocks of Hill Lands can be clearly seen. Above them, in the top centre, the builders are working on Purfield Drive, having completed Fidlers Walk. Wargrave was becoming a larger community.

grave Backwater.

CK'S POST CARD

STALE. ——— POSTKARTE.

(FOR ADDRESS ONLY.)

WARGRAVE

HOUSEBOATS. SHIPLAKE.

BACKWATER. THE CHURCH.

HIGH STREET. THE FERRY.

Christmas Greetings

Wish you were here . . .

Postcards were very popular, especially in the first half of the twentieth century. Many of the images in this book are drawn from the Wargrave Local History Society's collection.

As well as being the village's leading grocery store for many years, Burgis's also had a thriving café at one time.

Positioned between the tobacconist's and the Woodclyffe Hall, Talbot & Son are selling corn, seed and fodder.

Wargrave had branches of several national chains. The International Tea Company had been a household name since the 1870s. The adjoining tea parlour is in Timber Cottage, the oldest house in the village.

The Woodclyffe Hall in its early years - notice the stylish lamp post.

One of the boys is holding a jug, but we don't know whether his destination was The Greyhound or Burgis's grocery shop across the road.

The Bull is one of the oldest buildings in the village and has a fine set of oak beams. It also has chalk-lined cellars which are ideal for storing beer.

The heaviest traffic at the corner of the High Street and Church Street involves no more than two prams and an Austin Seven parked outside The Bull.

The Woodclyffe Hostel was built for the working people of the village, as an attractive alternative to the many local alehouses. It has served several purposes since it was opened in 1905 with a library and snooker club. Since then it has been used as a convalescent ward for wounded soldiers and a masonic lodge. There was also a public bath which was available to villagers who did not have one. Today it houses the Theatre Workshop costume store and is used for their rehearsals. Harriette Cooke Smith who provided the hostel would be pleased to see that the library and snooker club are still going strong, although she would not have approved of the club's licensed bar.

Harry Barker's bakery was established in 1824 at the junction of Church Street and Ferry Lane, near to the gate to Mill Green.

J. Richardson, Family Butcher & Poulterer, Wargrave.
Families waited upon daily for orders.

The original hooks for hanging the meat can still be seen today over a shop between the Woodclyffe Hall and the traffic lights. Next door there is a branch of W H Smith & Son.

The sign on the left is for the Wargrave Coffee Tavern. Prompted by the temperance movement, its aim was to attract working men away from the large number of alehouses in the village. The white building immediately beyond the Coffee Tavern was demolished to make way for the Woodclyffe Hall in 1900.

This photograph was taken in the early years of the twentieth century but the crossroads has always been a popular meeting point or place for a chat.

A customer's order book supplied by Rose & Bennett, whose dairy was next door to The Greyhound on the High Street. The redeveloped property is now known as Old Dairy Court.

A recent photograph of the forge at The Greyhound.

The view from School Lane across the High Street and down Church Street during the Edwardian period. Adjoining The Greyhound on the right is the blacksmith's forge which has been preserved.

Advertisements from a 1912 Parish Magazine give an idea of the wide range of businesses trading in the village.

Muddy going underfoot in Church Street, looking towards Mill Green.

Ferry Lane, or as it was also known, Free Ferry Lane.

The Wyatt family lived in the ivy-clad cottage in Church Street. The window with the awning was the coal office, where orders were taken and accounts paid.

The ladies' dresses and the pram suggest that the handwritten date on this postcard is probably correct.

Thirty years later, The White Hart has gained mock Tudor beams and you could fill up your car with petrol at the roadside pumps.

Perhaps the young man wearing the boater bought it from Sansom's shop and Post Office which is just behind him and next door to the bank.

Marian Sayers

The gateway with a small arch to the left of The White Hart marked the pathway up to the chapel which was built by The Countess of Huntingdon's Connexion, a small society of evangelical churches founded in 1783. The chapel was closed in 1981 and became a private house.

Boys and girls come out to play. The houses on the right are the first in a long row of cottages which face The White Hart. They are still there today, although they have since been painted white. Notice that the road surface is unmade.

Clearing the stable yard behind The White Hart.

Delivery traffic in the High Street.

The Henley Road, looking towards The St George & Dragon on the left.

The St George and Dragon

One side of the original inn sign depicts St George slaying the dragon; on the other side, our victorious patron saint is enjoying a well-deserved pint of best bitter.

The hotel's guests arrived by road or river.

Driving in the middle of the road was less of a problem in the 1900s.

Although some modernisation had taken place by the time this photograph was taken, the main entrance still opened straight onto the road.

Lord Barrymore

Standing at the junction of the High Street and Wargrave Hill, Barrymore was the home of Lord Barrymore who built a theatre on the other side of the road in 1788. It cost £300,000 and could seat an audience of 400 or more so that he could entertain his fashionable friends from London, including the Prince of Wales. It was the most modern and largest privately-owned theatre in England. Leading actors from London appeared, including Anthony Pasquin. A well-known clown at Covent Garden, Delphini, was engaged as Actor/Manager and lived at The Croft, a house at the end of The Bothy. There are persistent rumours of tunnels connecting Barrymore, the theatre and The Croft. The row of cottages in the High Street, often known as "The Barracks", was built to accommodate guests.

Lord Barrymore lived a short but hectic life, involving himself with some of the wilder elements of Georgian society. He was eventually declared bankrupt and the theatre was demolished. Even his death was dramatic; he accidentally shot himself whilst on military duty escorting French prisoners at Dover and was buried in Wargrave in an unmarked grave.

LORD BARYMORES THEATRE AT WARGRAVE.

Barrymore

A tale of two manors

Wargrave Manor was originally called Wargrave Hill, a play on words by Joseph Hill who had the house built in the 1780s. The list of families who have lived there over the past two centuries is varied and interesting. Among the more famous is Gertrude Jekyll, the eminent Victorian garden designer. The present owner is His Majesty the Sultan of Oman.

It is unclear whether the village had its own manor house in medieval times but it has been suggested that, if it did, Wargrave Court on Mill Green, pictured on the left, could have fulfilled that role. Parts of this lovely old house date from the fifteenth century and it would have been well sited, on the river bank and near to the mill. Being called a court might also indicate that it was the centre of manorial administration. It was at one time owned by Lord Braybrooke, Lord of the Manors of Wargrave, Waltham St Lawrence and Warfield but his manorial seat was at Billingbear.

Wargrave has many styles of domestic architecture, ranging from the grand to the quaint. Leafy Lane House, previously known as Greenwood Lodge and then Millwards, was one of the original farmhouses in the village; almost everyone coming from Twyford will have seen it on the right-hand side. Its imposing design is quite different to the small and charming Chapel House, seen below, tucked away on the Henley Road opposite its junction with Willow Lane. Originally it was known as Johannah Bailey's House.

Above we see a splendid pair of houses along Willow Lane, complete with wet boathouses. Roof repairs to Thatched Holme, below, would have kept the thatchers busy for a long time.

From military academy to hotel to private residence to modern houses

The Hill Lands development on Dark Lane gets its name from the large house which had stood on the site. It was originally the north block of a privately owned military academy founded in the 1880s but when the academy closed, the building became The Chiltern Towers Hotel, shown above in 1912. Perhaps as an echo of its military past, there is a flag flying. In 1909, Leonard Gower, one of the hotel's page boys, persuaded the vicar that a Boy Scouts troop should be formed, making it one of the earliest in the country.

The lower photograph shows that on conversion from hotel to private house, the main building was reduced in size on the right-hand side and the continuous roofed balcony was converted into individual balconies. The wing on the left-hand side of the hotel was demolished.

The White House in Ferry Lane was originally called Inverloddon and, during part of the time that it was owned by the Bellords family, Catholic Mass was celebrated here. Later, Mass was moved to Dr Black's boathouse until the village finally got its own Catholic church in 1963.

Pretty Corner, Wargrave.

These attractive old cottages are in The Bothy, the lane at the foot of Wargrave Hill. They back onto one of the two walled gardens which belonged to the manor. At one time, The Bothy was part of the main road to Crazies Hill but when Joseph Hill built what we now call Wargrave Manor, he closed the old road and created a new route up Wargrave Hill to give himself more privacy.

To EMMA WYATT & SONS,
DEALERS IN
COAL, COKE, AND WOOD,
WARGRAVE WHARF,
"GEORGE & DRAGON,"
WARGRAVE, BERKS.
ESTABLISHED 1845.

A working wharf

For many years, the well-known Wyatt family ran The St George & Dragon, as well as the adjoining boatyard and wharf, which was a landing stage for passengers and most of the village's river-borne freight, including coal. As can be seen in the 1897 photograph below, the ferry point was also used for sheep-dipping. Throughout many changes over the years, the hostelry has always provided welcome refreshment for visitors.

The ferry across to Shiplake provided a vital commercial and social link for hundreds of years, but now only operates during the annual regatta. The boatyard continued to offer a variety of craft for hire until the 1980s. Both these photographs and the upper one on the page opposite date from the beginning of the twentieth century.

Steaming along past The Willows in Wargrave.

The landing stage
at Ferry Lodge.

Punt and skiff hire proving popular at what we now know as Bushnells Marina. A boatyard was established by Henry Butcher in the middle of the nineteenth century and was bought by John Bushnell in 1917.

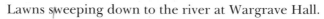
Lawns sweeping down to the river at Wargrave Hall.

Cape Farewell stands at the junction of the Loddon and the Thames and was built in about 1910. At one time it was owned by Lord Broadbridge, Lord Mayor of London. Its name was spelt *Faeirewell* on old maps, meaning "mouth of the beautiful stream".

An exercise in studied nonchalance at Shiplake weir.

Grand houseboats and houses were normal features during the river's social heyday.

Looking downstream from Shiplake Lock towards the timber-built railway bridge.

A touch of patriotic fervour and a fine canoe at Roselands in Willow Lane.

Downstream towards the Sailing Club.

Looking at The St George & Dragon
from an Oxfordshire point of view.

Tranquillity along the Hennerton Backwater.

Four men in a boat.

Camps Pool, or Puddle as it was sometimes called, is at the entrance to the Hennerton Backwater. It is the only part of the river visible to drivers coming through the village and has always been a popular place for fishing. The man operating the winch is smartly dressed for the photograph, complete with cap, suit and watch chain.

An elegant welcome to the Loddon.

The Loddon offers more peaceful moorings than the Thames.

The smallest and quietest of Wargrave's three rivers.

The huge popularity of our annual regatta is nothing new; it has been attracting large crowds since 1867 and draws entrants from far and wide. As a reminder of the former regular service, a passenger ferry at The St George & Dragon links the two villages, although now only for the two days of the event.

These two photographs are from Harriette Cooke Smith's albums and show us that regatta fashions were a little more formal in those days.

The majority of old postcards and other photographs of rowing on the Thames show it as largely a male activity. In contrast, here are Catriona, Mary, Pam and Jane, oarswomen from Wargrave Boating Club who are celebrating the opening of a new boathouse. The club was founded in the late 1940s, revitalised in the 1960s and is now a thriving centre of family boating.

Just enough headroom to explore the backwater.

A peaceful summer scene in the 1960s.

The St George & Dragon was featured in Jerome K Jerome's best-selling book, *Three Men in a Boat*, which has never been out of print since it first appeared in 1889. The number of boats registered on the Thames increased by fifty per cent in the following year.

The George and Dragon, Wargrave.

Vote for Gardner!

A lively political rally with a decorated "gunboat" drawn by a team of boys and accompanied by characters in costume. They are supporting Edward Gardner, the Conservative candidate in the 1910 General Election: their campaign was successful.

A regal group of ladies setting out for a cruise on the River Queen. Perhaps it's the effect of those hats, but they do look a little formidable and smiles are rather scarce. In the background on the left-hand side, we can just see some cattle grazing on the water meadows opposite The St George & Dragon.

Wargrave's first Girl Guide company was formed in 1919 and although we don't know the exact date of this photograph, the girl on the far left of the front row is Gladys Adby, a well-known lifelong resident of the parish who celebrated her 95th birthday in 2010.

The trophy for the winner of the annual WI Pancake Race on Mill Green being shown to the Revd John Ratings. It is now safely stored in the Society's archives.

Aren't they lovely? Let's hope that Phyllis, Mary, Mary, Dorothy and Gladys, the Wargrave Quaker Oats Girls, won a prize.

The Annual Sale

A very popular event in the 1950s and 1960s, much closer to the traditional jumble sale than today's rather more commercial charity shops. It also looks a lot livelier as villagers hunt for bargains.

The Piggott Schools

The three schools in Wargrave all take their name from Robert Piggott. Robert, a church-warden at St Mary's, had been married twice, but had no children. In 1796 he wrote his will, saying he wished to establish two schools for children of Wargrave, one for 20 boys and the other for 20 girls, and he detailed how they were to be run. After his death in 1798, his sister, Ann, added to the funds. The schools then occupied two cottages in the High Street, but in 1828 moved to Victoria Road, alongside the National School. Eventually, these schools all merged, moving to new premises built on School Hill in 1862.

By the early 1900s, the school had become overcrowded, so the 54 infants were moved from School Hill to the former poor law board school buildings in Victoria Road. The village population continued to grow, and the school leaving age was raised to 14, so the vicar, Canon Stephen Winter, proposed a new school for the older pupils, which opened in September 1940 - to serve not only Wargrave but also surrounding parishes, which Canon Winter had persuaded to support the project.

In 1963 the outdated Victoria Road premises were replaced by a new infant school in Beverley Gardens. The School Hill building, now only for junior-age pupils, was again full, so alterations were made to create more teaching space. At the Twyford Road site, classrooms and a canteen were added in the 1960s to cope with growing pupil numbers, and the grounds were enlarged and further buildings added as part of the preparations for the school becoming fully comprehensive from 1973.

The Robert Piggott Infant and Junior Schools and The Piggott School are therefore all Church of England schools, derived from Robert Piggott's original vision.

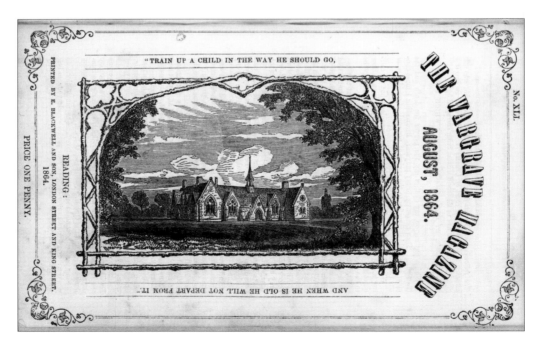

The Piggott School featured on the front cover of the Parish Magazine.

The Piggott Schools, from Chalk Pit, Wargrave

Junior school

The chalk pit was still in operation when the present school was built in 1862. The area to the left of the thatched hut is now the cemetery.

Infant school

The first infant school was in Victoria Road. The school moved in 1963 to new buildings in Beverley Gardens and its former site was used for Elizabeth Court and the surgery.

A building of huge importance to so many of Wargrave's sons and daughters.

One hundred years later, School Lane remains virtually unchanged.

Generations of village children have sat for the camera at the Junior or Infant school, wearing angelic expressions and wishing that the photographer would hurry up.

The Austen-Leigh family

Having lived as a boy at Scarletts, Kiln Green, the Revd Austen-Leigh became vicar of Wargrave in 1890 and in the photograph above we see him and his wife with two of their grandchildren.

The picture on the right shows Mrs Winifred Jenkin with Priscilla and Henry. Winifred's maiden name was, of course, Austen-Leigh. Henry was named after his grandfather.

For more details on the family's history and connection with Jane Austen, see *The Book of Wargrave*.

Miss Phyllis Baker

This well-known lady from Hare Hatch was descended from Sir Robert Baker, the Middlesex Police Magistrate after whom Baker Street was named. She was also related to the distinguished Young family whose home was at Hare Hatch House and who played a leading role in the provision of amenities for the local community. Phyllis and her cousin, Mabel Young, lived in Tag Lane at Shingleberry, which was built for them in 1938.

The Fuller Family

Frank

Ron and Polly

William was born in 1867 and became a highly respected member of the community. The Honour Certificate he received at junior school earned him a scholarship for secondary education. He was the foreman bellringer in his spare time and earned his living as a gardener. He shoulders his shovel as proudly as a guardsman would his rifle. His military bearing can be seen in his sons Frank and Ron.

A social highlight

Kitty Downs and Frank Wyatt were married in January 1890; it was clearly a grand local occasion with a fine selection of hats and dresses. Frank ran The St George and Dragon, where the group is seated facing the river. He also managed the boatyard and wharf.

Just the three of us . . .

This very early photograph shows the original wooden railway viaduct which carried the Great Western broad-gauge trains over the Thames at Wargrave.

A passenger train hauled by a typical tank-engine on its way to Twyford. The two small white buildings to the right of the engine are GWR corrugated iron huts. The right-hand one was a bicycle shed, the other was a parcels office.

The railway comes to Wargrave

It's hard to recognise that this is Wargrave station, looking towards Henley. The station is complete with two tracks, two platforms, a footbridge and buildings each side. It also had a signal box and a small siding for goods traffic. The railway first came to our village in 1857 when the Great Western broad-gauge line from Twyford to Henley-on-Thames was opened; the only problem was that the trains didn't stop. Despite pressure from residents, Wargrave's own station was not built until 1900 when Station Road was also constructed.

As with so many towns and villages, the coming of the railway had some lasting effects. Many goods such as newspapers, coal and fresh fish could be supplied more easily and villagers had quicker access to London and Reading. During the 1930s, camping coaches provided holiday accommodation. The station's decline began in 1961 when the line became single-track with one platform and the bridge was removed. In 1985 the remaining buildings were demolished and replaced by a simple shelter.

The age of the car had arrived. These motorists are happy to pose with their pride and joy at Pretty Corner, the junction of The Bothy and Wargrave Hill.

This somewhat dilapidated image shows a car in a similar condition. There's a definite lack of bodywork and seating. It is parked outside the former Infant School.

In 1930, a house-to-house collection raised £430 towards the cost of this Morris Commercial fire engine. Seated on the running board is William Easterling, a leading local builder who was closely associated with the brigade and who was always known as "The Governor".

These two gentlemen motorists and their magnificent machine are on the High Street, between the present-day garage and The White Hart, outside a house which served as a bank for many years.

Film star Robert Morley accompanies Lizzie French, the Village Festival Queen. He was always generous in his support of local events and often led the Parade, which frequently included historical or unusual modes of transport.

Royal Blue express coaches ran a regular service through the village for many years, but this restored example is not on its way to Westward Ho! in Devon as it is taking part in a Festival Parade and is being followed by the modern fire engine.

Knights and Ladies on horseback, plenty of foot soldiers and two damsels who do not appear to be in distress.

Terry Quantrill demonstrates his skill on the penny-farthing.

This cigarette card was one of a series given away by Cavanders in 1926 as part of their River Valleys series. The company has long since vanished from the British market but the brand is well known today in India.

River Valleys
A SERIES OF 108
Hand Coloured REAL PHOTOS
NO. 63

Wargrave Church

The old church at Wargrave was destroyed by fire on June 1, 1914, but rebuilt shortly after. Among the famous persons buried in or near the church was Day, the author of "Sandford and Merton," a native of the village. The register contains the following interesting record: "Oct. 10, 1666, collected £2:1:11 for the poor distressed Londoners by reason of the late lamentable fire."

ISSUED WITH
Army Club
CIGARETTES
CAVANDERS LTD
Established 1775

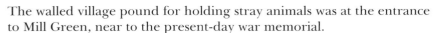

The walled village pound for holding stray animals was at the entrance to Mill Green, near to the present-day war memorial.

Springtime snow
in 1908.

Although the church before the fire in 1914 is immediately recognisable, there is no lych gate and the building to house the generator has not yet been built. In the 1970s it became the Hannen Room.

There are numerous clues to indicate that this picture shows the earlier church. They include the facts that there is no carved wooden rood screen at the chancel steps, the chandeliers are holding candles and all the pews have doors.

Looking over the fish pond to the north west of the church. Prior to 1914, the church tower was clad in ivy.

The clergyman "floating" above the church is the Revd Basil Staunton Batty, vicar of St Mary's from 1911 to 1914.

The Church Fire

The discovery in the early morning of Whit-Monday 1914 that the church was on fire marked one of the most notable events in Wargrave's history.

This was no accidental blaze as there was evidence that it had been deliberately started in several places with paraffin-soaked cloths, according to the diocesan architect's report, and it was strongly rumoured to have been the work of militant suffragettes. Three postcards were found by the vestry window bearing suffrage slogans - very similar to those found at a house fire caused by suffragettes at Windsor the same day. The fire was fierce, destroying all the timber and making much of the stonework unsafe. With flames coming from the top of the tower, the fire could be seen for miles around. The Wargrave fire brigade was soon on the scene, followed by the Henley and Wokingham brigades. Despite their efforts, the church could not be saved and the Wargrave firemen were left to damp it down into the late afternoon. By the valiant efforts of villagers, some items were rescued, notably the large heavy brass lectern presented in memory of a former vicar's widow which took four men to carry it out. The intense heat went up the tower, and after the clock struck at 3.15 am, the mechanism fell to the floor and the six bells, dating from 1668-88, were all destroyed.

The next weekend, a service was held in the open on Mill Green, and subsequently, a 'tin tabernacle' chapel was put up there. Despite it being wartime, the rebuilding was soon started, to a design by the diocesan architect, Mr W Fellowes Prynne. It involved taking the unsafe aisle pillars and south wall down to ground level, whilst the brick and stonework of the north wall and the tower were repaired. The opportunity was taken to lengthen the church by one bay at the eastern end. Some of the £15,800 total cost was covered through insurance, whilst the cost of many of the interior fittings, including the organ, was donated by villagers. The rebuilt church was consecrated on July 22nd 1916.

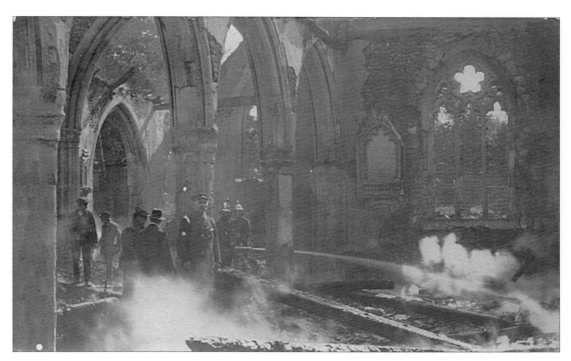

Firemen damping down the smouldering remains of the roof timbers.

The man leaning on the broom in the centre of the group is believed to be the vicar, the Revd Basil Staunton Batty.

The tower acted as a chimney for the fire, creating such intense heat that it partially melted the bells. The vicar and a policeman survey the scene, watched by a group of onlookers outside the west door.

Ladders and ropes being used to check and secure the badly damaged structure.

The remains of the clock mechanism lying at the foot of the tower.

Some of the bell metal recovered from the fire was used to make commemorative medallions. This one was cast for William Fuller, the Foreman Bellringer, and is shown actual size.

We shall rebuild!

William Fuller tolls the temporary bell on Mill Green.

Music for the open-air service was provided by a harmonium loaned by Mr Collins.

The choir processes from the 'Tin Tabernacle' to the reopening of the church on 22nd July 1916.

The cottages at the bottom of Victoria Road, or Jubilee Road as it was previously known, have not changed greatly, except that in this photograph they are thatched. In those days, postcards were sometimes used as Christmas cards.

The road became surprisingly narrow a little way up from the thatched cottages.

The Evelyn Home

The Convalescent Cottage for London Mothers and Infants had begun in Hertfordshire in 1908 to provide a fortnight's rest and holiday to London mothers and their new-born infants. It moved to Wargrave in 1913, where it became known as the Evelyn Convalescent Cottage, after its founder, Mrs Evelyn Murray. At that time, it occupied the house on the eastern corner of Victoria Road and East View Road where it could accommodate four mothers and babies.

The new home was opened by Princess Marie Louise in April 1926. She also often attended the annual Pound Day held in the grounds - a fete where people would donate a pound, or bring a pound of something to sell to help raise funds for the home.

Evelyn Murray was the wife of Sir John Murray, the publisher of J M Barrie's *Peter Pan* who gave the copyright income in perpetuity to Great Ormond Street Hospital in 1929. It is not surprising, therefore, that a close link was established between the Evelyn Home and Great Ormond Street Hospital. This was clearly shown when, at the Pound Day in July 1929, a Peter Pan Garden was opened. It had been given by Lady Murray as a memorial to her husband.

The home closed in the 1950s, and after use as a private residence, was replaced in about 1966 by the present East View Close.

Harriette Cooke Smith

Mrs Smith was the daughter of the Revd James Hitchings, who became vicar of Wargrave in 1826 when Harriette was two years old. She married William Smith, a wealthy London businessman and they bought a house in Wargrave. Over the years, Harriette became Wargrave's most generous benefactor and left a legacy which still affects almost everyone in the village. Her principal gifts included the Woodclyffe Hall, the allotments, the recreation ground, the Woodclyffe Hostel, the Woodclyffe Almshouses and the installation of electric lighting in St Mary's church. She also provided the village hall at Crazies Hill. Although this photograph is decidedly serious and creates a striking resemblance to Queen Victoria, Harriette was, by all accounts, lively, charming and artistically talented: a truly remarkable Victorian lady.

A historical detective story

Many of the photographs in this book which relate to Harriette Cooke Smith and some others too, come from her three personal albums which were saved from the Northampton council destructor at the eleventh hour by someone who noticed that although there were photographs from many places, a number were of Wargrave, where his colleague's in-laws live. He made enquiries and the story ended with the return of the albums to their home village where they were being examined by members of the Local History Society when one had a flash of inspiration and realised that the "HCS" monogram on the covers referred to Harriette.

On looking more carefully at the books lying on a table in the drawing room, it appears that one of them is a photograph album. It would be an amazing coincidence, but maybe, just maybe . . .

Exploring the wilder parts of her garden.

Woodclyffe

Harriette with her favourite
dog, Bant, who appears in a
number of photographs.

When William and Harriette Smith bought the house it was called Hillside but they quickly changed it to Woodclyffe, a name which became very well known to Wargrave residents, even 130 years later.

Woodclyffe and a partial view of the formal gardens.

The drawing room at Woodclyffe. The display cabinet in the upper photograph is still in place, although we understand that the current residents might have reduced the number of ornaments on display.

Harriette's widowed mother leaves her home at Orchard House on the High Street.

Two gardeners working at Orchard House.

These two photographs share a page in one of Harriette's albums so it seems likely that they were taken on the same occasion when visiting friends at Wargrave Hall. The upper one is simply captioned "Wargrave" and the lower one "From the lawn". Notice the discarded tennis racquet by the seat.

Which of you will it be today?

Harriette's handwritten caption is, "The Balcony - Woodclyffe".

Mr & Mrs Smith at their front door. We know that this photograph was taken later than the one on page 86 as the decorative plaque no longer says "Hillside".

This sketch is a creative representation of Queen Emma's Palace, a medieval building which is said to have stood on the site of the present Woodclyffe Hostel. Harriette's accompanying note says, "Drawn by my mother".

Heading south

The southern end of the High Street has always been a busy thoroughfare, linking Wargrave with Twyford and Reading. On the left-hand side, the sign of The Old North Star can be seen, it was not only a pub but also provided stabling. Directly opposite is The White Horse, another of the seven alehouses on the High Street at one time. Sitting in the road on a wheelbarrow wouldn't be recommended nowadays.

The pony and trap provided quick and effective light transport.

He might have only had one horsepower available, but this man's horse is a fine and powerful animal.

A few years later and the motor car is well established. For the benefit of pedestrians, the footpath is now better defined. The Old North Star, on the right, has become a private house.

Over the years, Twyford Road has been known as The Avenue and Southern Avenue. Until the 1950s it was lined with large trees. They were felled, on safety grounds, but it was an unpopular move with many residents.

WARGRAVE.—THE AVENUE

The boys are not making their way towards the Senior School, as it hasn't been built yet.

A long walk to Twyford.

Crazies Hill

This unusual name is said by some to come from an old word for buttercups. Folklore warned that smelling the flowers could possibly lead to madness. Firm evidence is in short supply.

A very early view of Crazies Hill School which first opened in July 1861 and remained in use until replaced by the present building in the 1960s.

The Crazies was originally built in 1790 as the Town Hall at Henley. It was dismantled and moved to Crazies Hill by Major Willis in 1898.

Rebecca's Well

In the mid-nineteenth century, there were few modern facilities for the people of Crazies Hill. They only had oil lamps or candles for lighting, there was no mains drainage and the water supply was a muddy pool around the spring in the woods, known as Rebra's Well. The Parish Magazine of the time said that the well had *"been long suffering from the action of the sun, so that, in summer, notwithstanding frequent clearings, a green floating mass of VEGETABLE matter - to say the least of it - was constantly defiling the water's fair surface, and insinuating itself into the pails and stomachs of the dippers"*.

Wargrave's new young curate, the Revd Grenville Phillimore, decided to help the villagers. He set about raising funds to have a proper basin fitted to the spring, which was done in July 1870. He also decided that Rebra was a form of the Biblical name Rebecca - chosen to be Isaac's wife when she went to the well to draw water. Although this seemed very appropriate, to many local people it became known as Phillimore's Spring. Later, a brick building was put up to surround the spring and basin, members of the parish subscribing the cost of £25. On the wall over the spring was added a scene showing Rebecca at the well, which was painted by Gertrude Jekyll, who lived for a time at Wargrave Hill, now known as Wargrave Manor. The painting was restored in relatively recent times.

A choice of transport at The Horse and Groom at Hare Hatch in the 1900s.

A meeting of the Ancient Order of Foresters at The Horse and Groom. The official title of the local Court, or branch, was "Pride of the Village". The Order was a Friendly Society with its origins dating back to Yorkshire in the 18th century. Members paid a few pence per week into a common fund which would provide some financial assistance if they or their families fell on hard times. Several are wearing regalia and the two on horseback have elaborate costumes. The proceedings are being overseen by a policeman standing at the back.

Yeldall Manor at Hare Hatch was built in the 1890s by Sir Arthur Schuster, an eminent scientist. This photograph was taken in the 1930s, when it had become The Convent of the Good Shepherd. In more recent times, the house has been used as an addiction rehabilitation centre.

The house behind The Queen Victoria at Kiln Green was originally another pub called The Queen Adelaide, which is why this area is often known as "The Two Queens".

Acknowledgments

The Editors are most grateful to all those who have helped in the preparation and printing of this book, whether through the contribution of images, information or ideas. They include:

Jean and Trevor Ackroyd	Richard Lloyd
David Ball	Lynda Mills
The Bird family	Mary Owen
Pam and Geoff Briggs	Helen Perry
John Dentry	Maureen Prince
Laila Embelton	Wendy Smith
Philip Emerton	Angela Sutton
Sandra Foster	

The Editor of *The Reading Chronicle* for kind permission to use the image of the Infant School on page 57.

Geoff Fisher of CPI Antony Rowe who gave valuable advice.

The Editors would also like to thank the members of the Wargrave Local History Society for their unfailing encouragement and support.

Index

Mill Green

Morning assembly

Morning assembly

PRAYERS

COMPILED BY HARRY TAYLOR FOR USE AT
KING JAMES'S GRAMMAR SCHOOL, ALMONDBURY
1951 - 1973

EDITOR
Roger Dowling

INTRODUCTION
Andrew Taylor

THE OLD ALMONDBURIANS' SOCIETY · KING JAMES'S SCHOOL · ALMONDBURY

Typeset in Perpetua and Gill Sans
Design: Roger Dowling
Print: MPG Biddles Ltd,
24 Rollesby Road,
Hardwick Industrial Estate,
King's Lynn,
Norfolk PE30 4LS

Published by
The Old Almondburians' Society
King James's School
Almondbury
Huddersfield HD4 6SG
www.oas.org.uk

ISBN 978 0 9557314 1 9

Also available from
The Old Almondburians' Society:

A History of King James's Grammar School in Almondbury (1963)
Gerald Hinchliffe

King James's Grammar School in Almondbury: An Illustrated History (2008)
Roger Dowling and John A Hargreaves

Both publications available online at www.oas.org.uk

OREWORD

MORNING ASSEMBLY and morning prayers are amongst the
memories which many of us have of our schooldays. Whilst these prayers
may have fallen on some deaf ears, for others they were like recurring
'melodies' which set the tone for the day.

Harry Taylor's morning prayers not only reflected his deep faith but also
his conspicuous respect for all who worked with him and for the students
who were in his charge.

Harry was a friend who helped me with his wise counsel when I was
writing the School history many years ago. He rang me regularly and
invariably laced his good advice with humour and sharp wit. I remember
that on one occasion he reminded a Speech Day audience that whilst Henry
Ford had declared that 'history was bunk', at King James's Grammar School
'the bunk' was history.

On another occasion in one of my rough drafts I had included a
humorous reference from Easther's glossary concerning a local man who
had found a somewhat sacrilegious use for his bible. In no uncertain terms
Harry 'ordered' me to take it out. "If you leave it in," he said, "I will be in
trouble with the Vicar."

The original idea of publishing these prayers came from Bryan
Hopkinson, a former chairman of the Old Almondburians' Society. Harry's
son Andrew has provided a stylish and witty introduction to this fascinating
collection of Harry's favourite prayers that I am sure the Gaffer himself
would have enjoyed reading. I know that he has been greatly helped in this
by the recollections of his brother Richard and his sister Alison.

Harry was a fine man whose influence during his years as headmaster has
remained memorable. This collection of his 'melodies' will remind many of
their days at Almondbury. Well done, Harry. Whence comes another?

Gerald Hinchliffe

MANY YEARS AGO, Harry Taylor's grandchildren used to be told that the impressive domed building that they could see on their left as they crossed the Sheffield flyover, decorated in the evening dark by thousands of fairy lights, was a shrine built on the spot where their grandfather was born. Other people might call it the Meadowhall Shopping Centre, but they knew better.

That story may not be precisely true in every particular, but it is probably close enough. He was born in 1909 in Kimberworth, South Yorkshire, now a suburb of Rotherham but back in the early twentieth century a village in its own right with its own church, shops and primary school – where his father, Henry Taylor, was headmaster. He was one of three children, with an older and a younger sister. An old copy of Daniel Defoe's Robinson Crusoe bears witness to his tenacity and reading ability, even as a small boy: inscribed in the front "From Father and Mother, Aug. 10th 1916," along with his name, it has

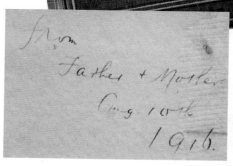

427 tightly-packed pages of small print. These were the days before abridged versions, children's editions, or even illustrations, but he claimed later in his life to have sat and read it from cover to cover over the week or so following his seventh birthday. Even allowing for the possible exaggerations that old men may be prone to, it is an astonishing achievement.

A certificate from Kimberworth Council School marking the results of the 1919 entrance examinations for Rotherham Grammar School shows an embarrassingly smug image of a boy holding a flag on which Harry Taylor's name has been inked in, with a top mark of 91.4%. He was marked out from the start as a bright boy. More interesting, though, is the headmaster's signature – H. Taylor. When, later in his life, Harry Taylor had his own sons at King James's, he could look back on his earlier experience as a small boy of having his father in the headmaster's study.

From Rotherham to Doncaster

By and large, his Rotherham Grammar School reports were the sort of thing one would expect of a future headmaster, despite the occasional misconduct marks scattered around – a smattering of '1sts' and 'Very goods' over the next eight years. Maybe his 'strange lack of interest throughout' in English and History during 1926 was because he was

Climbing the ladder: Harry Taylor showed his early promise as he took the entrance examinations for Rotherham Grammar School in 1919

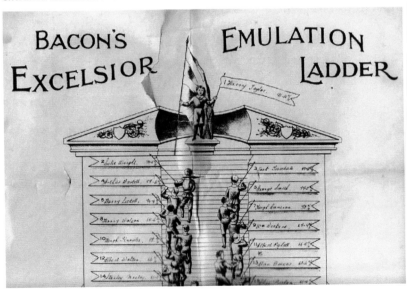

> My last conversation with Harry Taylor as a pupil of Almondbury Grammar School before going off to University included a piece of advice about women. It was interspersed with several 'umphs' and made the observation that when he went to buy a new cricket bat he didn't buy the first one he was offered but tried a few before making his selection.
>
> I have always remembered that conversation. He may have given the same advice to many others but he certainly made it special to me.
>
> Paul Balderstone (1954-62)

playing so much cricket – apart from captaining the school cricket and football teams, and winning the annual athletic competition, he was playing regularly for the team at the nearby Maltby Main colliery. Whatever the reason, that brief hiccup seems not to have held him back: apart from his academic and sporting successes, he was appointed Captain of the School for three years in a row – a great honour, but surely a lack of imagination by the headmaster!

From Rotherham Grammar School, he went off to St John's College, Oxford to read modern history, and took a Second Class degree. He returned to the north straight away to take up a post as junior history master, first at Doncaster Grammar School for one term's teaching practice, and then for a year at Queen Elizabeth's Grammar School in Mansfield, before returning to Doncaster for a permanent post teaching history and English in 1933. In Doncaster, he got not only valuable initial experience as a schoolmaster, but also a wife: it was while he was teaching there that he met Jessica Anderson, a Manchester Classics graduate born in Leeds who was teaching Latin in nearby Maltby, and who would later carve out her own role at King James's as the Gaffer's wife. On the evening they got engaged, he had been on his way to a Labour Party meeting: later in her life, she liked to either boast or confess, depending on your point of view, that their engagement probably kept him out of the Party.

From Doncaster to Almondbury

Like Rotherham Grammar School, and like King James's, Doncaster was a school with a long history, dating back at least to the early 14th century. Harry Taylor knew the school already through having played cricket against it while he was at Rotherham – Doncaster's school magazine has reports of him as an aggressive 18-year-old opening batsman in 1927 making 49 in the first match of the season between the two schools and 'scoring freely' to reach 64 in the second. He was quickly involved in sport at Doncaster as well, becoming Vice-President of the School Cricket Club. He was also in charge of the School Library, a role which an anonymous correspondent in the school magazine described as 'not very difficult ... but increasingly irksome.' A sketch of him carrying out his duties with characteristic energy seems to bear this assessment out.

Feet up: Harry carries out his new duties as librarian at Doncaster Grammar School with 'characteristic energy'

The Librarian - D.G.S.

'After my interview in the Town Hall in 1953, Harry Taylor introduced himself in a friendly and self-effacing fashion, and then took me to the School, which until then I had not seen. It was unbelievably impressive in the June sunshine. In the Study, with the rattle of teacups, there was a very relaxed gathering; Fred Hudson was there, along with the Chairman of the Old Almondburians' Society, a man called Ronnie Parkin with an enormous handlebar moustache. These three were clearly the significant figures of the school.

So began the most memorable and satisfying period of my teaching life, 15 years in all. Mr Taylor always had a special interest in the teaching of Latin: his wife and mine were both classicists, from the same university, and he wanted Latin to play a full part in the grammar school curriculum.

An historian by training, he was the right man at the right time to deal with the discovery of the Charter and the Statutes, along with the true name and declared purpose of the School.

He took prayers for Assembly from the Statutes, and his historical sense imbued many boys with pride in the School. The Taylor Dyson Library was significant, and I was privileged to be the first librarian, further enlarging a good collection of local history books. Here Sixth Formers were encouraged to take their first steps in research. He set an example himself, by transcribing the Almondbury Parish Registers for the Record Series of the Yorkshire Archaeological Society, in whose archives the Charter had been found.

His leadership in all areas was quiet and imperturbable. He had the foresight to sponsor the formation of the Scout Troop, one of the most successful enterprises of those years. He fostered Drama and the unique Jacobean Society, and visits to the Balkans, to France and to Italy, all contributing to the rounded education in which he firmly believed. Such an education was inevitably crowned with academic success.

Jim Toomey (staff 1953-1968)'

His career, like that of many young men of his generation, was interrupted by the War, and he left Doncaster in 1940 to join the RAF, serving as Education Officer on several bomber stations in Lincolnshire. Apart from his day-to-day duties, he also acted as Defending Officer in

Continued on page 8

5

Harry Taylor

1. King James's Grammar School

2. School cricket field

3. All Hallows' Church

4. The Woolpack

5. 15 Westgate, (the Taylors' first home)

6. 37 St Helen's Gate (the Taylors' later home)

Note: the photograph, taken in 2007, shows a number of additions to the School and village after Harry Taylor's time at Almondbury

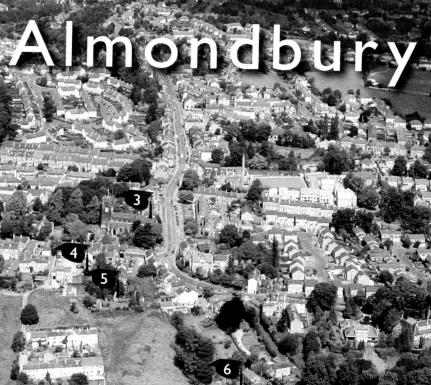

Almondbury

Continued from page 5

a number of Courts Martial, an experience which seems to have fired his interest in the law. When the war was over, he studied law and was called to the Bar at the Middle Temple in 1948.

By then, he was back at Doncaster, by now Senior History Master and father of a four-year-old son and a year-old daughter. When he left, the tribute in the school magazine summed up the impression that

Not guilty: although called to the Bar, Harry never practised as a barrister

his seventeen years at the school had left behind:

> *His sympathetic understanding at all times of boys' difficulties won for him a very natural love and respect; this disposition and a delightful sense of humour always contributed to the happy atmosphere of the Masters' Common Room.*

He did not know, as he arrived at what was then Almondbury Grammar School in 1951, that he was entering the school where he would spend the rest of his career. It was not until a couple of years later, walking up St Helen's Gate at the end of a long day, that he realised that he had found the place that he wanted to be – an ancient school, nestling in a beautiful valley, with traditions from the past and potential for the future. There was All Hallows' Church to satisfy one side of his character, and the Woolpack opposite to satisfy another. There was even a historic connection with his own childhood, he found out later – Archbishop Thomas Rotherham, who was instrumental in the rebuilding of All Hallows' in the fifteenth century, was the same Thomas Rotherham who had founded Rotherham Grammar School in 1483.

There was a busy, thriving community in Almondbury and in the town, plenty of opportunity to play cricket, and a garden close to the house in Westgate where he was living. He was in the right place.

A Lucky Headmaster

Napoleon used to say that his generals needed above all to be lucky, and much the same quality is important for headmasters as well. Within a few months of taking over, Harry Taylor heard the news that Fred Hudson and his eagle-eyed team from the School Surveying Society, visiting an exhibition at Leeds, had found the original School Statutes and the Charter with the seal of King James I.

It was an inspiring start to his headship, particularly as he was dedicated to the idea of giving pupils at Almondbury what he saw as the best aspects of public school education. In this, he was building on the work of his three predecessors, Horace Vessey Moore, John Baldwin, and the

Reunited: the return of the long-lost Charter was an exciting moment for the new headmaster. Second master Fred Hudson (left) led the party that spotted it at an exhibition in Leeds in 1952

> Imagine the scene. The old Art Room on the 'N. Corridor'. A very junior teacher, one Dave Bush, is taking a 2nd form class for English. It's the last day of a Test Match and at a critical stage. There's a radio on at the back of the class so that we can 'keep in touch with the score' while the lesson continues. The door opens and Headmaster, Harry Taylor walks in. The floor of the Art Room refuses to open up. HT delivers his message and as he leaves, nods in the direction of the radio, turns to the red-faced DB and says 'Delighted to see you empathising with your pupils, Mr Bush. An 'umph' and he was gone. It would have been beyond belief to be told that in a little over ten years' time I would be sitting in Harry Taylor's chair as Acting Headmaster during the Autumn Term, 1973. What a pair of shoes (size 12?) to try to fill. I take only a 6 so never really mastered his art of kicking shut the bottom left hand drawer of his desk. It retained the scuff marks for many a year.
>
> When I had the unenviable task of organising his farewell at the end of the Summer Term, 1973, I summed him up under the perhaps surprising title of 'Cricket and Chrysanthemums'. Yet I felt that was Harry Taylor, a generous gentleman and a very humane headmaster.
>
> Dave Bush (staff 1961-1996)

great Taylor Dyson – the School already had a house system, based on the names of the ancient local families of Dartmouth, Fenay, Jessop and Siddon; it had an active Old Almondburians' Society; and now it had a Charter that emphasised its long history and its ancient traditions.

In Almondbury, it said, there should be a grammar school for ever, 'For the instruction of boys in good learning and virtue'.

It was only a matter of time – seven years, in fact – before the school's name was changed to reflect its history, and AGS became King James's Grammar School. Among the traditions that flourished were the Founders' Day service, with its carefully placed apostrophe to reflect, as all new boys were told, the fact that the School had not one founder but several, and the annual formality of Speech Day in the Town Hall.

By this time, he had a third child – whether his birth was a cele-

(Above) All Hallows' Church in Almondbury has historic links with the School.
Harry Taylor leads the annual Founders' Day procession to the church

(Below) Harry Taylor's first Speech Day at Huddersfield Town Hall was in March
1952 when the guest speaker was Old Almondburian Sir Harold Himsworth,
secretary to the Medical Research Council

HARRY TAYLOR: CRICKETER

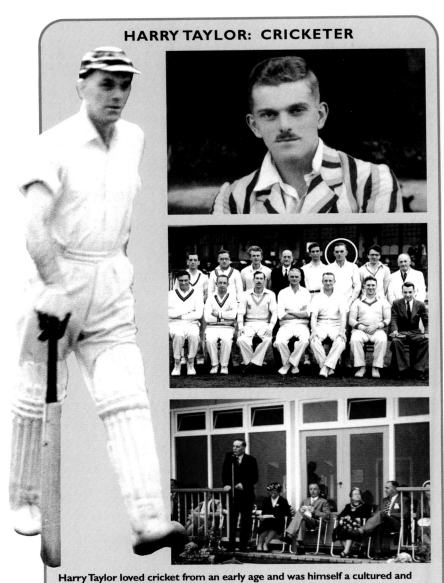

Harry Taylor loved cricket from an early age and was himself a cultured and elegant batsman and a bowler of wily leg spin.
(Top) University days: the moustache did not survive
(Middle) Playing for Mexborough Cricket Club in 1946
(Bottom) The opening of the new school cricket pavilion in 1958 by the Countess of Scarbrough

> After commencing teaching at the grammar school in September 1959, Mr Taylor* would frequently ask me on the Monday morning, about my cricket experience on the previous weekend. On one particular occasion I arrived in the old Physics Lab, pre-assembly, with four stitches below my chin – a souvenir of my latest game. Mr Taylor enquired as to the origin of the wound. On replying that I had been hit by the ball whilst batting, he retorted that my bat should have been put to better use.
>
> Mr Taylor was very keen to further inter-school cricket, in addition to School and House cricket. I was umpiring in a School match against Huddersfield College on one occasion when he enquired of the scorer, from the boundary, "Bowler's name?" The pre-arranged reply in an equally loud voice, "Trueman, sir", had the desired shock effect on the incumbent batsman as he perished to the very next ball.
>
> On one occasion in the mid-sixties, at Almondbury Casuals Cricket Club, I went out to bat with Mr Taylor already at the wicket. Desperately anxious to get off the mark I called him for a quick single. "No, get back!" he replied. Before play could be resumed he walked towards me, informing me in a stern voice, "I never run singles!"
>
> *Jack Taylor (staff 1959-1997)*
>
> *From respect, I only ever addressed Harry Taylor as 'Mr Taylor' or 'Headmaster/Head'; other staff likewise. I can only remember Fred Hudson calling him 'Harry', and George Beach on social occasions. How times have changed!

bration of Harry Taylor's appointment as Headmaster nine months earlier, or just a reflection of the fact they he and Jessica now felt they could afford it, is not certain. Both the new baby and his elder brother would eventually go the School. Jessica, meanwhile, had her own role there as well. Along with the other wives of what was, in those early days, an exclusively male School staff, she organised the annual Wives' Dinner on the same night as the Old Almondburians' Dinner. She also, less officially, would warn the occasional grammar school boy whom she saw smoking or otherwise misbehaving in St Helen's Gate that the Gaffer was just around the corner.

FAMILY MAN

(Top) Wedding Day, 1941
Bottom left) Richard and Alison in 1947 (Bottom right) Andrew in 1956

Morning Assembly

And of course, there was the Morning Assembly – a legal require-
ment, but a ceremony by which Harry Taylor set great store. It always
followed the same pattern, with the whole School drawn up in rows in
the gym – or, on particularly sunny summer days, on the old tennis
court outside the Library. They ranged from bright-eyed little boys in
short trousers (Yes – short trousers) at the front to cynical old Sixth
Formers, who were just about starting to shave, at the back. There
would be a quiet buzz of side-of-the-mouth conversation for as long as
you could avoid the eyes of the staff and prefects standing along the
side, then a hush as the Gaffer himself approached up the corridor.

> In Form 6 I took History with Harry Taylor. We were a select group of six, as I remember. One day, Harry arrived late. He explained that he had been with people who had come to check the dry rot that was spreading in the old building. We all sat down in his study, and Harry said, "And talking of dry rot, I have here your essay for this week, Byram."
>
> When the Inspectors came – there was no Ofsted, then – Harry asked me to read one of my essays. I read an essay on the wars of Louis IV: long, passionate, gauche, clumsy perhaps, imbued with youthful pacifism and Methodism, not firm foundations for historical scholarship. There ensued an argument between me and the Inspector. I may have gone too far.
>
> Nevertheless, Harry received a good report – he showed me – and I was mentioned in despatches.
>
> *Reggie Byram (1946-54)*

There was the morning hymn, one or two announcements – maybe the cricket team had beaten Huddersfield New College, or some "guttersnipe" had been writing on a wall somewhere, and it had to stop – and then the prayers.

There were occasional special assemblies, of course: once a year, for example, in accordance with an endowment dating back to the 17th century, there was the payment of one red rose to the Nettleton Charity. As Headmaster, Harry Taylor made the presentation, and as a Trustee of the charity, he received it as well. He had also, incidentally, grown it in his own garden too.

And then, when he retired, 22 years after his arrival, his last moments as Headmaster were spent in front of the boys in a final end of term assembly.

There were presentations to be made, of course – but he wanted it to be as near as possible a normal assembly, he said. They would sing his favourite hymn – one he had not been allowed to have at his wedding, he noted, with a slightly reproachful glimpse at his wife, who had come as a guest. Since it was "Fight the good fight", her reluctance was probably understandable. Then there would be three prayers that he particularly liked — St Augustine's "Oh Lord our Saviour, who hast warned us that thou wilt require much of those to whom much is given", the prayer that the School should be "as a field which the Lord hath blessed, that whatsoever things are true, pure, lovely and of good report may here for ever flourish and abound", and Sir Francis Drake's prayer outside Cadiz harbour, that when embarking on "any great matter", we should know "that it is not the beginning but the continuing of the same until it be truly finished, which yieldeth the true glory".

You didn't have to be particularly religious to find something to think about in those prayers, and you would have had to be deaf to miss the catch in his voice as he read them to the School for the last time.

The Gaffer probably would not have known what was meant by the expression 'new man', and he certainly wouldn't have thanked you for calling him one if he had. But he had no problem in acknowledging his own emotions. "Forty-five years ago," he told the boys on that day in 1973, "I was a head boy making a presentation much like this one." He had noticed then that the senior master receiving the gift had tears in his eyes, he said, and he had wondered why.

"After 45 years, I understand it. What you people have done, and what you have said through your head boy, have really moved me considerably. You may see tears drop from the Headmaster's eyes now — a rather interesting thing to tell your friends and your children when you have them, that you saw someone weep on the platform." And then, since he had a sense of humour, he paused. "We'll try to manage without it," he added.

In the Right Place

By the time he left his Study for the last time, Harry Taylor knew that he had been not just the 24th Headmaster of the grammar school that King James had promised should exist in Almondbury 'for ever', but also the last. National and local politicians and the Education Act paid no account to the wishes of a 17th century monarch, and King

> I began my teaching career at King James's Grammar School in September 1973 as a probationary Teacher of French. My first meeting with Harry was in the previous February when I arrived at the school from teaching practice at Doncaster Grammar School for my first ever interview.
>
> I was ushered into the study where I came across a relaxed man in a gown, puffing on a pipe with his feet on the table. After a few minutes' conversation about my qualifications, experience of travel abroad and why I wanted to teach, Harry then noted from the application form that I was a keen sportsman – especially football and cricket. After finding out my preferred position in both sports, Harry then turned the interview into an in depth discussion on the state of Yorkshire County Cricket Club and Huddersfield Town. He then proceeded to offer me the position – much to my delight – and I am eternally in his debt for allowing me to spend 15 happy years at King James's!
>
> Bob Field (staff 1973-1987)

James's was starting the gradual process of change to a Sixth Form College.

He made no secret of his dislike for the comprehensive education policy, and he felt that his idea that bright boys from ordinary backgrounds should be given access to the very best education was being betrayed, but he genuinely wished the new King James's well. He remained an Almondburian, he wrote in his last notes in the School magazine, "and when the bell rings in St Helen's Gate for the new term, it will toll for me too".

He had a busy retirement: he had already established himself as a local cricketer with the Almondbury Casuals Club, although the quick singles of his youth had given way first to slow singles and then to innings consisting entirely of fours. He was well known as an imaginative and witty speaker at sports and other dinners all over Yorkshire, and he spent several years as the local representative of the British Council,

looking after foreign students in Huddersfield. Jessica joined him in that, as she did in his co-authorship, along with Fred and Joyce Hudson and a number of other local worthies, of "The Village on the Hill" a booklet of local Almondbury history. Jessica also helped him over several years in the transcribing of the All Hallows' Church parish registers from the 16th century onwards.

All Hallows, with its historic links with the School, was important to him in several ways – the place where his daughter and later one of his grandsons were married, and where he regularly read the lesson. And if his readings were occasionally followed by a Sunday lunchtime pint in the Woolpack across the road – well, that was one of the things that had attracted him to Almondbury in the first place.

But whatever else he did, he was always first and foremost the Headmaster or the former Headmaster of King James's. He had spent his life in the right place.

RAYERS

King James's Grammar School.

———

Prayers

for

Morning Assembly etc

———

H. Taylor

Prayer from the ancient Statutes

We look up unto thee, O Lord, from whom
cometh every good and perfect gift,
beseeching thee to direct, assist and bless
all the labours of our mind. Illuminate
our understandings, O Father of Lights, and
lead us unto right apprehensions of all things.
Endue us with that humility and soberness
of mind which thou delightest to reward
with more of thy gifts and graces. Bestow
upon every one of us a discerning spirit,
a sound judgment, and an honest and good
heart, sincerely disposed to employ all the
talents which thou hast or shalt intrust us
withall, to thy honour and glory, and to
the good of mankind.   For which end,
we beseech thee to excite our thirst after good
learning and useful knowledge. And especially
enrich us with the treasures of that inspired
wisdom contained in thy Holy Scriptures, which
are able to make us wise unto salvation.
That growing in understanding and

goodness, as we grow in years, our profiting may be apparent unto all men. Through Jesus Christ our Lord.

Prayer from the ancient Statutes

O Almighty Lord, and merciful Father,
maker of heaven and earth, which of thy free
liberality givest wisdom abundantly to all
that with faith and full assurance ask it of
thee / , beautify by the light of thy heavenly
grace the towardness of our wits, / the which
with all powers of nature thou hast poured
into us ; / that we may not only understand
those things which may effectually bring us
to the knowledge of thee, / and the Lord Jesus
Christ our Saviour, / but also with our whole
hearts and wills constantly follow the same / ,
and receive daily increase through thy bountiful
goodness towards us, as well in good life
as doctrine ; so that thou, which workest all
things in all creatures, mayest make thy gracious
benefits shine in us to the endless glory and
honour of thine immortal majesty ;
for Jesus Christ his sake // , in whose name and
words we further call upon thee, saying
     Our Father etc.

God grant me (us)

Serenity to accept the things I (we) cannot change,
Courage to change the things I (we) can,
And wisdom to know the difference.

3

25

For the School

4 O Lord our Saviour, who hast warned us that
Thou wilt require much of those to whom much
is given; grant that we whose lot is cast in so
goodly a heritage, may strive together the more
abundantly .... to extend to others what we so
richly enjoy; and as we have entered into the
labours of other men, so to labour that in their
turn other men may enter into ours, to the
fulfilment of Thy holy will, and our own
everlasting salvation; through Jesus Christ
our Lord.

— St. Augustine 4ᵗʰ Cent

5 O God, we pray thee to send thy blessing
upon this School, and grant that by the help of
thy Holy Spirit we may strive with one heart and
mind to make this place more and more pleasing
to thee, for the honour and glory of thy Son
our Saviour Jesus Christ

— F. A. Sill

26

For the School.

Almighty God, in whom we live, and move, and have our being, make this school as a field which the Lord hath blessed, that whatsoever things are true, pure, lovely, and of good report, may here forever flourish and abound. Preserve in it an unblemished name, enlarge it with a wider usefulness, and exalt it in the love and reverence of all its members as an instrument of thy glory, for the sake of Jesus Christ our Lord.

For the School

O God and Father of us all, who givest to thy
children light and life and happiness, we pray
thee for thy blessing on this day : sanctify it,
we beseech thee, by thy constant presence :
in labour let us always work to thee, in leisure
never grieve thy Holy Spirit. Control our affections,
hallow our thoughts, inspire our hopes, quicken
our prayers and praises ; and may we be so
bound each to other in all true fellowship, and
to thee in all faithful service, that in the
love of the brotherhood, we may perfect the love
of God; through Jesus Christ our Lord.

— Dr. James.

We beseech thee, O Heavenly Father, to prosper with
thy blessing, and enlighten with thy holy wisdom
all who teach and all who learn in this our School.
Grant that, rejoicing in the knowledge of thy
truth, we may worship thee and serve thee
all the days of our life.

Through Jesus Christ our Lord

For the School

O God, our heavenly Father, from whom cometh every good and perfect gift, we beseech thee to bestow thy blessing on our School. We praise thee for the heritage into which we have entered, and pray thee to make us worthy to maintain and strengthen all that is good in our traditions. Give to all who work here the true love of knowledge which makes all study a discovery and a joy. May the spirit of loyalty and devotion bind us all more closely together, that we may labour not for our own advantage, but for the common good. X May thy wisdom guide and prosper our work and games, our clubs and societies, that we may grow in the love of all that is true and honest and of good report. And when we go out into the world, may we carry with us the ideal and the power of service, which thou dost give us in thy Son Jesus Christ our Lord

— Book of Prayers for Students

For the School

Let us give praise to Almighty God that at all times he has been pleased to impart knowledge and wisdom to those who have sought after him.

Let us remember his many blessings bestowed upon this ancient school and upon those who through the centuries have laboured here.

Let us remember our founders, benefactors, teachers, and scholars who by their gifts and devotion have, in this place, made notable contribution to godliness and sound learning.

And let us pray that we may be worthy of our inheritance

Through Jesus Christ our Lord.

Visit, we beseech thee, most gracious Father, this School with thy protection. Let thy blessing descend and rest on all who belong to it. Guide us here, and hereafter bring us to thy glory;
Through Jesus Christ our Lord

30

For the School

12

Continue to give, O God, thy blessing
to this school, that nothing may tarnish
its honour or break its comradeship.
May thy presence keep all in true peace
so that separately and together we may
serve Thee with all our powers.

13

Thankfully remembering its past;
bearing its present before Thee; trusting
and hoping for its future, we bring
our school to Thee. May thy blessing
be always upon it, and may we who
share its life make it part of thy
Kingdom of Heaven on earth, and so
give praise and glory to Thee, and
joy to others

14 Morning

O Lord our heavenly Father, almighty and
everlasting God, who hast safely brought us
to the beginning of this day; defend us in the
same with thy mighty power; and grant that
this day we fall into no sin, neither run
into any kind of danger; but that all our
doings may be ordered by thy governance,
to do always that is righteous in thy sight;
through Jesus Christ our Lord.

　　　　- Book of Common Prayer

15 Almighty God, who fillest all things with thy
presence, we meekly beseech thee, of thy
great love, to keep us near unto thee this day;
grant that in all our ways and doings
we may remember that thou seest us, and
may always have grace to know and perceive
what things thou wouldst have us to do,
and strength to fulfil the same,
through Jesus Christ our Lord

　　　　Ancient Collect, 5ᵗʰ Century

Morning

Enter with us, O God our Saviour, upon the
life of this day. Be thou our companion
in all that we have to do. In our difficulties
grant us guidance. In our weakness send
us strength. Help us to do our duty
earnestly, to bear our troubles bravely, and
to serve thee and our fellows with wisdom
and cheerfulness; through Jesus Christ
our Lord.

H. Bisseker

O Loving Father, our eternal Friend,
may we never forget or dishonour thee
this day; but in all places and in all
          tasks.
occupations remember thy presence
and cherish thy love;
for Jesus Christ's sake.

                    - Dean Vaughan.

Morning

18 O God, our Father, help us this day to speak
and to do only such things as will leave no
regret. Grant us reverence for all that is good;
teach us to hate all that is selfish and base.
In our dealings with our fellows, inspire
in us the spirit of courtesy and goodwill.
And make us masters of our own life, strong
to control our desires and resolute to match
our action to our highest thought;
through Jesus Christ our Lord

         — H. Bisseker

19 Grant us, O Lord, to pass this day in
gladness and peace, without stumbling and
without stain, that, reaching the eventide
victorious over all temptation, we may
praise Thee, the eternal God, who art
blessed and dost govern all things,
world without end.

         — Ancient Spanish

Morning

Let thy blessing, O Lord, rest upon our
work this day. Teach us to seek after
truth, and enable us to attain it,
but grant that as we increase in the
knowledge of earthly things, we may
grow in the knowledge of thee, whom
to know is life eternal;
through Jesus Christ our Lord

- Thomas Arnold 1795-1842

Morning

O God, our Father, who dost desire us
to love and to serve one another, and who
hast created us for fellowship with Thee and with
our fellow men, grant unto us all through
this day, the gifts and the graces which will
make us easy to live with.

Grant us courtesy, that we may live every
moment as if we were living at the Court of the King.

Grant us tolerance, that we may not be
so quick to condemn what we do not like
and what we do not understand.
[Grant unto us considerateness, that we may think
of the feelings of others even more than of our own]

Grant unto us kindliness, that we may
miss no opportunity to help, to cheer, to
comfort and to encourage a brother [man]

Grant unto us honesty, that our work
may be our best whether there is anyone
to see it or not . . . . .

Through Jesus Christ our Lord
   — Barclay

Morning

O God our Father, equip us with these
gifts of Thine which will enable us to live
aright today and every day.

Grant unto us the faith which can accept
the things it cannot understand, and which
will never turn to doubt.

Grant unto us the hope which still hopes
on, even in the dark, and which will
never turn to despair

Grant unto us the loyalty which will be
true to Thee, even though all men deny Thee,
and which will never stoop to compromise.

Grant unto us the purity which can
resist all temptation, and which never
can be turned from the straight way

Through Jesus Christ our Lord

Morning

Into thy hands, O Lord, we commit
ourselves this day. Give to each one of us
a watchful, a humble and a diligent
spirit, that we may seek in all things
to know thy will, and when we know it,
may perform it perfectly and gladly,
to the honour and glory of thy name

Morning

O God our Father, deliver us this day from all
that would keep us from serving Thee.

Deliver us from all coldness of heart; and grant
neither hand nor heart remain shut to someone's need.

Deliver us from weakness of will; from the
indecision which cannot make up its mind; from
the irresolution which cannot abide by a decision
once made; from the inability to say No
to temptation

[Deliver us from all failure in endeavour;
from being too easily discouraged; from
giving up and giving in too soon; from
allowing any task to defeat us because
it is difficult.]

Grant us this day the love ~~that~~ which is generous
in help; the determination which is
steadfast in decision; the perseverance
which is enduring unto the end;

Through Jesus Christ our Lord
— Barclay

Thanksgiving

Almighty God, we thank thee for rest and health; for work to do, and strength to do it; and for all the surroundings of our life that make it desirable and enjoyable. Do thou raise our thoughts and purify our aspirations. Strengthen our wills, we beseech thee, on the side of what is right and good, and against what is wrong and evil; through Jesus Christ our Lord

O Lord, as thy mercies do surround us, so grant that our returns of duty may abound; and let us this day manifest our gratitude by doing something well pleasing unto thee; through Jesus Christ our Lord.

— Archdeacon Edward Lake, 1641.

Thanksgiving

Almighty God, Father of all mercies,
we thine unworthy servants do give thee most
humble and hearty thanks for all thy goodness
and loving-kindness to us and to all men.
We bless thee for our creation, preservation and
all the blessings of this life; but above all for
thine inestimable love in the redemption of the
world by our Lord Jesus Christ; for the means of
grace and for the hope of glory. And we beseech
thee, give us that due sense of all thy mercies,
that our hearts may be unfeignedly thankful,
and that we may show forth thy praise, not
only with our lips, but in our lives; by giving
up ourselves to thy service, and by walking
before thee in holiness and righteousness
all our days; through Jesus Christ our Lord,
to whom with thee and the Holy Ghost be all
honour and glory, world without end.

       - Book of Common Prayer.

Confession

Almighty and most merciful God,
we acknowledge and confess that we have
sinned against thee in thought, and word,
and deed; that we have not loved thee with
all our heart and soul, with all our mind
and strength; and that we have not loved
our neighbour as ourselves.   We beseech thee,
O God, to be forgiving to what we have been,
to help us to amend what we are, and of thy
mercy to direct what we shall be, so that
the love of goodness may ever be first in our
hearts, and we may follow unto our lives'
end in the steps of Jesus Christ our Lord.

      —John Hunter.

Forgive, O Lord, our many shortcomings,
our coldness of heart, and wandering
of thought in thy service, and keep us
evermore in thy fear and love,
through Jesus Christ our Lord.

Confession

Almighty God, our heavenly Father,
who of thy great mercy hast promised
forgiveness of sins to all them that
with hearty repentance and true faith
turn unto thee, have mercy upon us;
pardon and deliver us from all our sins;
confirm and strengthen us in all
goodness, and bring us to everlasting
life; through Jesus Christ our Lord.

      — Book of Common Prayer, adapted.

Forgive us, O Lord, all that we have done
amiss and all the good that we have failed
to do. Endue us with thy Holy Spirit, that
we may have grace to please thee and
power to serve thee all the days of
our lives. Through Jesus Christ our Lord.

Confession

Almighty and most merciful God,
we acknowledge and confess that we have
sinned against thee in thought, and word,
and deed; that we have not loved thee with
all our heart and soul, with all our mind
and strength; and that we have not loved
our neighbour as ourselves.   We beseech thee,
O God, to be forgiving to what we have been,
to help us to amend what we are, and of thy
mercy to direct what we shall be, so that
the love of goodness may ever be first in our
hearts, and we may follow unto our lives'
end in the steps of Jesus Christ our Lord.

— John Hunter.

Forgive, O Lord, our many shortcomings,
our coldness of heart, and wandering
of thought in thy service, and keep us
evermore in thy fear and love,
through Jesus Christ our Lord.

Dedication

O God, who hast commanded us to be
perfect, as thou our Father in heaven
art perfect, put into our hearts, we
pray thee, a continual desire to obey
thy holy will.   Teach us day by day
what thou wouldst have us do, and
give us grace and power to fulfil the same.
May we never from love of ease decline
the path which thou dost appoint, nor
for fear of shame turn away from it;
for the sake of Jesus Christ our Lord.
               — Henry Alford.

Teach us, good Lord, to serve Thee as
Thou deservest; to give and not count the
cost, to fight and not heed the wounds,
to toil and not seek for rest, to labour
and not ask for any reward, save that
of knowing that we do Thy will.
               — St Ignatius Loyola (1491 – 1556)

Dedication

Let us pray that God will accept and use us as an instrument of his purpose. Let us in our thoughts put him first and ourselves second, fixing our minds less on our will and needs than on his infinite wisdom and power, praying that he will purge out of our life all that hinders his action in and through us, that he will make us selfless, singlehearted and strong, Christ's faithful soldiers and servants unto our lives' ends; through Jesus Christ our Lord.

Dedication

Father of all wisdom, understanding and true strength, we beseech thee look mercifully upon us, and send thy Holy Spirit into our hearts: that when we must join to fight in the field for the glory of thy holy name, then, being strengthened with the glory of thy right hand, we may manfully stand in the confession of thy faith, and of thy truth, and continue in the same unto the end of our life; through our Lord Jesus Christ.

— Nicholas Ridley 1500 - 1555

O God, who hast commanded that no man should be idle, give us grace to employ all our talents and faculties in the service appointed for us; that, whatsoever our hand findeth to do, we may do it with our might.

— James Martineau, 1805 - 1909

Dedication

39   O Lord God, when Thou givest to Thy servants to endeavour any great matter, grant us to know that it is not the beginning but the continuing of the same, until it be thoroughly finished, which yieldeth the true glory.

— Sir Francis Drake   c. 1545-96

40   O Lord, Thou knowest how busy I must be this day. If I forget Thee, do not forget me.

— Jacob Astley 1579-1652

41   O Lord, let us not live to be useless, for Christ's sake.

— John Wesley, 1703-91

42   These things, good Lord, that we pray for, give us Thy grace to labour for.

— Sir Thomas More 1478-1535

Dedication

O Lord, give thy blessing, we pray thee,
to our daily work, that we may do it
in faith and heartily, as to the Lord and
not unto men. All our powers of body
and mind are thine, and we would fain
devote them to thy service. Sanctify them,
and the work in which they are engaged;
let us not be slothful but fervent in spirit;
and do thou, O Lord, so bless our efforts
that they may bring forth in us the
fruits of true wisdom. // Teach us to seek
after truth, and enable us to gain it; ....
through Jesus Christ our Lord

       — Dr. Thomas Arnold.

Character and Guidance

For a Clean Heart

44 O eternal God, who hast taught us by thy holy word that our bodies are temples of thy Spirit, keep us, we most humbly beseech thee, temperate and holy in thought, word, and deed, that at the last we, with all the pure in heart, may see thee, and be made like unto thee, in thy heavenly kingdom, through Jesus Christ our Lord.

— Bishop Westcott.

For Ready Obedience

45 Make us of quick and tender conscience, O Lord; that understanding, we may obey every word of thine this day, and discerning, may follow every suggestion of thine indwelling spirit;

Through Jesus Christ our Lord

— Christina Rossetti.

For Pure Thoughts and Intentions

Almighty God, unto whom all hearts be
open, and from whom no secrets are hid,
cleanse the thoughts of our hearts by the
inspiration of thy Holy Spirit, that we may
perfectly love thee, and worthily magnify
thy holy name; through Christ our Lord
        — Bishop Leofric 11ᵗʰ Cent; B. of C.P.

For Purity of Heart

O most merciful and gracious God, we
beseech thee to hear our prayers, and to
deliver our hearts from the temptation of
evil thoughts, that, by thy goodness,
we may become a fitting habitation
for thy Holy Spirit; through Jesus Christ our Lord.

Grant that no word may fall from me
against my will unfit for the present need.
        — Pericles.

Character and Guidance

For Truthfulness

Almighty God, who hast sent the
spirit of truth unto us to guide us into
all truth, so rule our lives by thy power,
that we may be truthful in word, deed,
and thought. O keep us, most merciful
Saviour, with thy gracious protection,
that no fear or hope may ever make us
false in act or speech. Cast out from
us whatsoever loveth or maketh a lie,
and bring us all to the perfect
freedom of thy truth; through Jesus
Christ our Lord.
                    — Bishop Westcott

For Guidance

O God, forasmuch without thee, we are
not able to please thee, mercifully grant that
thy Holy Spirit may in all things direct and
rule our hearts; through Jesus Christ our Lord.
                    — Book of Common Prayer.

Character and Guidance

O heavenly Father, subdue in us
whatever is contrary to thy holy will.
Grant that we may ever study to know
thy will, that we may know how to
please thee. Grant, O God, that we may
never run into those temptations which
in our prayers we desire to avoid.
O Lord, never permit our trials to be
above our strength;
Through Jesus Christ our Lord.

For Humility and Unselfishness

O Lord, give us more charity, more
self denial, more likeness to thee.
Teach us to sacrifice our comforts to others,
and our likings for the sake of doing good.
Make us kindly in thought, generous in deed,
gentle in word. Teach us that it is better
to give than to receive, better to forget
ourselves than to put ourselves forward;
Through Jesus Christ our Lord.

53 Make us eager, O Lord, to share the
good things which you give us.
Give us such a measure of your spirit
that we may find more joy in giving
than in getting. Make us ready
to give cheerfully without grudging,
secretly without praise, and
sincerely without looking for gratitude.

54 Give us a sense of humour, Lord.
Give us the grace to see a joke;
To get some happiness from life,
And pass it on to other folk.

General Intercession

Look in mercy, O Lord, on all around us.
Bless this school and neighbourhood in which
we live. Bless our Queen and country.
Guide our rulers, that everything may be
ordered according to thy will for thy glory
and the welfare of all men. Give us peace
and such prosperity as may be good for us.
Look in mercy on the sins and miseries
of men, and help us in some way to
minister to their needs;

through Jesus Christ our Lord.

For our Country

Lord, bless this kingdom, that religion
and virtue may season all sorts of men;
that there may be peace within our gates,
and prosperity in all our borders. In time
of trouble guide us, and in peace may we
not forget thee; and whether in plenty
or in want, may all things be so ordered,
that we may patiently and peaceably seek
Thy Kingdom and its righteousness, the
only full supply and sure foundation
both of men and states; so that we may
continue a place and people to do Thee
service to the end of time. Through
Jesus Christ our Lord.

- William Laud 1573 - 1645

For the Queen

Almighty God, the fountain of all
goodness, we humbly beseech thee to bless
our Sovereign Lady, Queen Elizabeth,
the Parliaments in all her dominions, and
all who are set in authority under her;
that they may order all things in
wisdom, righteousness, and peace, to the
honour of thy holy Name, and the good of
thy Church and people; through Jesus Christ
our Lord

— Prayer Book 1928 (modified)

Eternal God, who rulest in the kingdoms of men:
Grant, we most humbly beseech thee, honour and safety
to our Sovereign Lady, Queen Elizabeth; peace throughout
the Commonwealth of her peoples; promotion to true
religion; encouragement to learning and godly
living; a patient service to the concord of the world;
and, by all these, glory to thy holy Name;
for his sake, to whom thou hast given all power
in heaven and earth, our Lord and Saviour Jesus Christ.

— Jeremy Taylor 1613-67, adapted.

For Assistance in Daily Work

59

O God, who knowest that we are not sufficient of ourselves to help ourselves, but that all our sufficiency is of thee, assist us with thy grace in all our work. Direct us in it by thy wisdom, support us by thy power, that doing our duty diligently, we may bring it to a good end; through Jesus Christ our Lord.

For Scouts

Almighty Father, help us to remember that thy only Son our Lord Jesus Christ was once a boy, full of life and eagerness, happy, content, obedient. Grant that we may try to follow his example, so that we may be a blessing to all around us. Help us to overcome temptation as he overcame it, to be unselfish and willing to help others as he was.
Give us strength to be humble followers in his heroic path, so that we may finally live with him in heaven.

Grant this for Jesus Christ's sake.

Give us, O Lord, a steadfast heart,
which no unworthy thought can drag downwards,
an unconquered heart, which no tribulation
can wear out; an upright heart, which
no unworthy purpose may tempt aside

Bestow upon us also, O Lord my God,
understanding to know thee,
diligence to seek thee,
wisdom to find thee,
and a faithfulness that may finally
embrace thee;
through Jesus Christ our Lord

— St Thomas Aquinas (1225-74)

<u>For Help in Learning.</u>

O Lord Jesus Christ, eternal wisdom
of the Father, Thou who hast added to man's
nature the benefit of teachableness, memory
and understanding, hear our prayers.

Give the help of Thy grace to our own natural
endeavours, that we may the more readily learn
true knowledge and sacred learning,
which shall serve Thy glory.;

For Thy Name's sake.

— used by John Hampden at Thame G.S.

63 O Lord our God, grant us grace to desire
thee with our whole heart ; that, so desiring
we may seek, and, seeking, find thee ;
and so finding thee, may love thee ;
and loving thee, may hate those sins
from which thou hast redeemed us.
Through Jesus Christ our Lord
                    - St. Anselm.

64 O Lord, we beseech thee to give courage
to thy children, wisdom to the perplexed,
endurance to sufferers, fresh vigour
and interest in life to those who have
lost heart, a sense of thy presence to
the lonely, comfort to the dying, and a
clear vision of thy truth to those who
are seeking thee ;
        Through Jesus Christ our Lord

May the strength of God pilot us.
May the power of God preserve us.
May the wisdom of God instruct us.
May the hand of God protect us.
May the way of God direct us.
May the shield of God defend us.
May the host of God guard us against the
    snares of evil and the temptations of the world.
May Christ be with us
Christ before us.
Christ in us.
Christ over us
May thy salvation, O Lord, be always ours
this day and forever more
            - St Patrick (389-461)

O most merciful Redeemer, Friend and Brother,
May we know Thee more clearly,
Love Thee more dearly,
Follow Thee more nearly:
For ever and ever. Amen
        - St Richard of Chichester 1197 - 1253

65

66

63

O Lord Jesus Christ, who art the Way,
the Truth, and the Life, we pray Thee
suffer us not to stray from Thee, who art
the Way, nor to distrust Thee, who art
the Truth, nor to rest in any other thing
than Thee, who art the Life.

   Teach us by Thy Holy Spirit what to believe
what to do, and wherein to take our
rest. For Thy Name's sake, Amen

                    - Erasmus   c. 1466 - 1536

Grant to us, O Lord, to know that which is
worth knowing, to love that which is worth
loving, to praise that which pleaseth thee most,
to esteem that which is most precious unto
thee, and to dislike whatsoever is evil in
thy eyes. Grant us with true judgment
to distinguish things that differ, and above all
to search out and to do what is well pleasing
unto thee, through Jesus Christ our Lord.
                    - Thomas à Kempis

Lord, make us instruments of thy peace.
Where there is hatred, let us sow love;
Where there is injury, pardon;
Where there is doubt, faith;
Where there is despair, hope;
Where there is darkness, light;
Where there is sadness, joy.

O Divine Master, grant that we may
not so much seek to be consoled as to
console; to be understood as to
understand; to be loved as to love;
for it is in giving that we receive;
it is in pardoning that we are pardoned;
and it is in dying that we are born
to Eternal Life.

— St. Francis of Assisi

70 O God, who lovest a cheerful giver,
help us to find happiness in the things which
we can do each day for those around us,
especially for those in great need.

Teach us that the joy of giving is the real
joy of living.

We ask it through Jesus Christ, who showed
us that to live we must love and serve.

71 O God, teach us to be considerate in our
demands, courteous in our speech, and
generous in our gratitude; always showing
to all men the honour that is their due.

72 Almighty God, give us grace, we pray thee
to hallow every gift and improve each talent
thou hast committed to us, that with a cheerful
and diligent spirit we may ever serve thee;
and whatsoever we do, do all in the name of
Jesus Christ our Lord.

Give us grace and courage, O God, to follow the guiding of our conscience, no matter what the cost, and help us to be ready to give ourselves in willing service for others

Through Jesus Christ our Lord

73

O Lord, as we go to our work this day, help us to take pleasure in it. Show us clearly what our duty is; help us to be faithful in doing it. May all we do be well done, fit for thine eye to see. Give us enthusiasm to attempt, and patience to perform. When we cannot love our work, may we think of it as thy task, and make what appears unlovely beautiful through loving service.

Through Jesus Christ our Lord.

74

For the Peace of the World.

75

Almighty God, from whom all thoughts of truth and peace proceed: Kindle, we pray thee, in the hearts of all men the true love of peace, and guide with thy pure and peaceable wisdom, those who take counsel for the nations of the earth; that in tranquillity thy kingdom may go forward, till the earth is filled with the knowledge of thy love; through Jesus Christ our Lord

— Bishop Paget of Oxford (1851 – 1911)

76

Almighty God and most merciful Father, who wouldest have the kingdoms of the world become the kingdom of thy Son Jesus Christ: Bestow thy blessing, we beseech thee, upon all who labour for peace and righteousness among the peoples; that the day may be hastened when war shall be no more, and thy will only shall govern the nations upon earth; through Jesus Christ our Lord.

— Armistice Day, 1931

For All Men.

O God, the creator and preserver of all mankind,
we humbly beseech thee for all sorts and conditions
of men; that thou wouldest be pleased to make
thy ways known unto them, thy saving health unto
all nations. More especially, we pray for the good
estate of the Catholic Church; that it may be so
guided and governed by thy good Spirit, that
all who profess and call themselves Christians
may be led into the way of truth, and hold the
faith in unity of spirit, in the bond of peace,
and in righteousness of life. Finally, we
commend to thy fatherly goodness all those,
who are any ways afflicted, or distressed,
in mind, body, or estate, ... that it may
please thee to comfort and relieve them,
according to their several necessities, giving
them patience under their sufferings, and a
happy issue out of all their afflictions.
And this we beg for Jesus Christ his sake.

— Bishop Gunning 1614-84; B. of C. P.

Parliament

O Merciful God and Father, forasmuch as no counsel can stand, nor any can prosper, but only such as are gathered in thy Name :

We pray thy Divine Majesty so to incline the hearts of them that are elected to the High Court of Parliament, that their counsels may be subject in true obedience to thy holy word and will. Graft in them, we beseech thee, good minds to conceive, free liberty to speak ; and grant to us all a ready and quiet consent to such wholesome laws and statutes, as may declare us to be thy people, and this Realm to be prosperously ruled by thy good guiding and defence ; through Jesus Christ our Lord.

—Prayer of 1585 (shortened and slightly altered)

Friendship.

O Lord, who hast provided for us many
friends, giving to us freely and without
thought of return: Grant that we, remembering
that we are debtors, may render to others the
kindnesses which we ourselves have received;
for Jesus Christ's sake.

Grant us, O Lord, loyalty of heart, that as
we demand that others should be faithful to us,
we also may be faithful to them;
for Jesus Christ's sake.

79

80

Sir Winston Churchill

Let us give thanks to Almighty God for the life of Winston Churchill, Knight, and for his service and inspiration to our country

O Lord God Almighty, we give thee most humble thanks for those who have dedicated their lives for the freedom of mankind — and especially Winston Churchill, whom we remember today. Grant, O Lord, that their memorial depart not away so long as the word endureth; nor the people cease to tell their praise before Thee, who gavest them courage, and dost accept the sacrifice; through thy Son, our Redeemer, Jesus Christ.

⟨ Drake's prayer⟩

Be mindful, O Lord, of the souls of thy servant who has gone before us with the sign of faith, and who rests in the sleep of peace. To him, O Lord, and to all who rest in Christ, mercifully grant a place of refreshment, of light, and of peace; through Jesus Christ our Lord

The Commons' Prayer

Almighty God, by whom alone Kings reign,
and Princes decree justice; and from whom alone
cometh all counsel, wisdom and understanding;
We thine unworthy servants, here gathered
together in thy Name, do most humbly beseech
thee to send down thy Heavenly Wisdom from
above, to direct and guide us in all our
consultations: And grant that, we having thy fear
always before our eyes, and laying aside all private
interests, prejudices and partial affections, the
result of all our counsels may be the glory of thy
blessed Name, the maintenance of true Religion and
Justice, the safety, honour and happiness of the Queen,
the publick welfare, peace and tranquillity of the
Realm, and the uniting and knitting together
of the hearts of all persons and estates within the
same, in true Christian Love and Charity
one towards another, through Jesus Christ
our Lord and Saviour.

— 17th century or earlier.

73

Evening

O God, from whom all holy desires, all good counsels, and all just works do proceed; give unto thy servants that peace which the world cannot give; that both our hearts may be set to obey thy commandments, and also that by thee being defended from the fear of our enemies, may pass our time in rest and quietness; through the merits of Jesus Christ our Saviour

      — Book of Common Prayer.

Lighten our darkness, we beseech thee, O Lord, and by thy great mercy defend us from all perils and dangers of this night; for the love of thy only Son, our Saviour, Jesus Christ.

      — Book of Common Prayer

For the Forgotten

Let us never forget, O Lord, the innocent victims of man's inhumanity [to man]: [the millions who were destroyed in the gas chambers and in the holocaust of Hiroshima and Nagasaki, and the few who survived, scarred in mind or body]; the uncounted numbers all over the earth who will never have enough to eat, [and who, through poverty or ignorance, must watch their children die of hunger]; the lepers and the cripples, and the countless others who will live out their lives in illness or disease for which they are given no relief; all who suffer because of their race or their creed or the colour of their skins; and all the children who, in their weakness, are torn from their parents [and robbed of the loving care which is their birthright]. Help us, as we go [unheedingly] about our daily lives, to remember those who silently call to us, and to remember also that, though the need of those in distress is so vast and of such an infinite complexity, it is by the steadfast effort of each one of us individuals that it must be conquered.

—contemp. American

Evening.

88

Save us, O Lord, waking; guard us
sleeping; that awake we may watch
with Christ, and asleep we may
rest in peace

— Breviarium Romanum 1570

89

keep us, Lord, so awake in the duties
of our callings that we may sleep in thy
peace and wake in thy glory

— John Donne 1573 - 1631

Christmas

Eternal Father, who by the birth of thy beloved Son, Jesus Christ, didst give thyself to mankind: grant that, being born in our hearts, he may save us from all our sins, and restore within us the image and likeness of our Creator, to whom be everlasting praise and glory, world without end.

Grant us, O Lord, such love and wonder that with humble shepherds, wise men, and pilgrims unknown, we may come and adore the Holy Babe, the Heavenly King; and with our gifts, worship and serve him, our Lord and Saviour Jesus Christ.

Beginning of Term.

O Lord, let thy blessing rest upon us throughout this term. Give us health of body, clearness of mind, patience and perseverance. Unite us in the desire to follow Christ and unselfishly to serve one another. May all that we do, in work and play, be done to thy honour and glory.

For the sake of Jesus Christ our Lord.

For those leaving School

We commend, O Lord, unto thy fatherly
care thy servants about to leave this School,
beseeching thee that thy loving kindness
and mercy may follow them all the days
of their life.   Succour them in temptation,
preserve them in danger, assist them
in every good work, and keep them ever
in the right way.
        And grant, O Father, that by thy
merciful aid, we may so walk before thee
in this life, that we may all meet again
in thy eternal kingdom;
through Jesus Christ our Lord.

End of Term.

O God, we offer our thanks for all thy goodness to us during the term and ask for thy blessing on our holidays.

Guide us and guard us, and grant that, wherever we may go, we shall think and speak and act as true followers of thy Son Jesus Christ.

Beginning of Term

To thee, O Lord, we humbly dedicate this Term. Sanctify both our labours and our pleasures, that hallowed by thy Holy Spirit we may undertake and do only that which is pleasing to thee. Grant us courage to overcome difficulties and thy special grace to withstand all temptations. Ever abide with us, O Lord, and grant that in all things we may worthily use the time which thou hast given us to thy honour and glory; through Jesus Christ our Lord.

<u>Closing Prayers.</u>

96

The grace of our Lord Jesus Christ,
and the love of God, and the fellowship
of the Holy Spirit, be with us all evermore

God Almighty bless us with his Holy Spirit;
guard us in our going out and coming in;
keep us ever steadfast in his faith, free

97

from sin, and safe from danger;
through Jesus Christ our Lord.

May the blessing of God Almighty, the Father,
the Son, and the Holy Ghost, rest upon us
and upon all our work and worship done

98

in his Name. May He give us light to
guide us, courage to support us, and
love to unite us, now and for evermore

99

End of Term.

Forgive us, Merciful Father,
all that we have done amiss and
all that we have failed to do aright
throughout this Term. Bring to full
fulfilment the good that we have
learned and done. Grant us in our
holidays refreshment, happiness
and health, preserve us from all
misfortune and save us from all sin,
through Jesus Christ our Lord.

Closing Prayers.

Grant, O Lord, that what we have heard with our ears we may believe in our hearts; and what we believe in our hearts we may practise in our lives. through Jesus Christ our Lord

Let the words of my mouth, and the meditation of my heart, be acceptable in thy sight, O Lord, my strength and my redeemer

OTES ON THE PRAYERS

PRAYERS FROM THE ANCIENT STATUTES

1. We look up unto thee…
2. O Almighty Lord…

The School Statutes were found to be in the safe custody of the Yorkshire Archaeological Society when the Charter was 're-discovered' in 1952.

Drawn up between 1695 and 1700 during the headship of Rev Abraham Walker.

FOR THE SCHOOL

4. O Lord our Saviour… (St Augustine)

Saint Augustine (354-430), also known as Augustine of Hippo, was the greatest of the Latin Church fathers. his most celebrated works were Confessions and De Civitate Dei (On the City of God), a study of the relationship between Christianity and secular society.

5. O God, we pray thee… (F H Sill)

Possibly Father F H Sill, sometime headmaster of Kent School, Connecticut.

7. O God and Father of us all… (Dr James)

Possibly Francis James (1581-1621), Latin poet — Westminster, ChCh, Oxford. MA 1605, DD 1614. Rector of St Matthew's, Friday St, London c1616.

9. O God, our heavenly Father… (Book of Prayers for Students)

A book of prayers published around 1915 by the Student Christian Movement.

MORNING

14. O Lord our heavenly Father... (Book of Common Prayer)
The Book of Common Prayer is the short title of a number of related prayer books used in the Anglican Communion. A Book of Common Prayer with local variations is used in churches inside and outside the Anglican Communion in over 50 different countries and in over 150 different languages.

15. Almighty God, who fillest all things with thy presence... (Ancient Collect)
Possibly derived from 'Ancient Collects and other prayers' (1862) by William Bright MA, Fellow of University College, Oxford.

16. Enter with us, O God our Saviour... (H Bisseker)
Harry Bisseker was Headmaster of The Leys School, Cambridge, 1919-1934.

17. O Loving Father, our eternal Friend... (Dean Vaughan)
Charles John Vaughan (1816-1897) was fellow of Trinity College, Cambridge and headmaster of Harrow School from 1844-1859. An eloquent preacher, he was Dean of Llandaff from 1879.

18. O God, our Father... (H Bisseker)
See 16.

20. Let thy blessing, O Lord...
(Thomas Arnold)
Thomas Arnold (1795-1842) was a historian, classicist and educator. His reforming headmastership of Rugby School (1828-1841) is described in the novel Tom Brown's Schooldays. *He was the father of the Victorian poet Matthew Arnold.*

Thomas Arnold

21. O God, our Father, who dost desire us to love... (William Barclay)
William Barclay (1907-1978) was a Church of Scotland minister and Professor of Divinity and Biblical criticism at Glasgow University. He became known as an author and radio and television presenter who was determined to make biblical scholarship available to non-academic readers.

24. O God, our Father, deliver us this day… (William Barclay)
See 21.

26. O Lord, as thy mercies do surround us… (Edward Lake)
Dr. Edward Lake was Archdeacon and Prebendary of Exeter, and chaplain and tutor to the future Queens Mary and Anne, daughters of the Duke of York, later King James II.

THANKSGIVING
27. Almighty God, Father of all mercies (Book of Common Prayer)
See 14.

CONFESSION
28. Almighty and most merciful God… (John Hunter)
Congregationalist preacher at Trinity Church, Glasgow and King's Weigh House Chapel, London. According to the Oxford History of Christian Worship, his Devotional Services (1880) "provided Congregationalists with a full, dignified worship book that was independent of the Book of Common Prayer".

30. Almighty God, our heavenly Father… (Book of Common Prayer)
An adapted extract; see 14.

DEDICATION
34. O God, who hast commanded… (Henry Alford)
Henry Alford (1810-1871) was an English churchman, theologian, textual critic, scholar, poet, hymnodist, and writer. His chief fame rests on his four-volume monumental edition of the New Testament in Greek which occupied him from 1841 to 1861.

35. Teach us, good Lord… (St Ignatius Loyola)
Ignatius of Loyola (Basque: Iñigo Loiolakoa, Spanish: Ignacio de Loyola) (1491-1556) was a Spanish knight from a Basque noble family, hermit, priest since 1537, and theologian who founded the Society of Jesus (Jesuits) and was its first Superior General. Ignatius emerged as a religious leader during the counter-reformation. Loyola's devotion to the Catholic Church was characterised by unquestioning obedience to the Catholic Church's authority and hierarchy.

37. Father of all wisdom... (Nicholas Ridley)

Nicholas Ridley (c. 1500-1555) was an English Bishop of London. Ridley was burned at the stake, as one of the Oxford Martyrs, during the Marian Persecutions, for his teachings and his support of Lady Jane Grey. Ridley is remembered with a commemoration in the Calendar of Saints in some parts of the Anglican Communion on 16 October.

38. O God, who hast commanded... (James Martineau)

James Martineau (1805-1900) was an English religious philosopher influential in the history of Unitarianism. For 45 years he was Professor of Mental and Moral Philosophy and Political Economy in Manchester New College, the principal training college for British Unitarianism.

39. O Lord God, when thou givest... (Sir Francis Drake)

The Elizabethan sea captain and privateer Sir Francis Drake (1540-1596) who completed the second circumnavigation of the world in 1580. He was second in command of the English fleet that defeated the Armada eight years later.

Sir Francis Drake

40. O Lord, thou knowest how busy I must be... (Jacob Astley)

Jacob Astley, 1st Baron Astley of Reading (1579-1652) was a Royalist commander in the English Civil War. This battle-prayer at the Battle of Edgehill has become famous: it was followed promptly with the order "March on, boys!" The troops on both sides were poorly trained and claimed the battle to be a victory, but the outcome was inconclusive and it would take a further three years of civil war before the Royalists lost to the Parliamentarians.

41. O Lord, let us not live to be useless… (John Wesley)
John Wesley (1703-1791) was an eminent Church of England clergyman and theologian.With his brother Charles, he was influential in starting the Methodism movement with his famous open-air preaching sessions.

42. These things, good Lord… Sir Thomas More)
Sir Thomas More (1478-1535) was a lawyer, author, renaissance humanist and Lord Chancellor of England under King Henry VIII. His opposition to Henry's decision to split from the Roman Catholic Church led to his conviction and execution for treason in 1535. His book Utopia describes a fictional island and its idealised way of life.

43. O Lord, give thy blessing… (Dr Thomas Arnold)
See 20.

CHARACTER AND GUIDANCE
For a Clean Heart
44. O eternal God… (Bishop Westcott)
Bishop of Durham, 1890-1901. He was known not only as a biblical scholar and theologian who had served as Regius Professor of Divinity at Cambridge University, but also as a social reformer and staunch supporter of the co-operative movement.

For ready obedience
45. Make us of quick and tender conscience… (Christina Rossetti)
English Victorian poet (1830-1894) whose most famous collection was Goblin Market and Other Poems *(1862). She wrote romantic and devotional poetry for both adults and children. Her poem* In the Bleak Midwinter*, set to music after her death, became a popular Christmas carol.*

Christina Rossetti

For Pure Thoughts and Intentions

46. Almighty God, unto whom all hearts be open... (Bishop Leofric)

Leofric (before 1016–1072) was a medieval Bishop of Exeter where worked to increase the income and resources of his cathedral, both in lands and in ecclesiastical vestments. He was a bibliophile, and collected many manuscripts; some of these he gave to the cathedral library, including a famous manuscript of poetry, the Exeter Book.

For Purity of Heart

48. Grant that no word... (Pericles)

Pericles (c. 495 – 429 BC) was an Athenian general, statesman and orator. Pericles promoted the arts and literature; it is principally through his efforts that Athens holds the reputation of being the educational and cultural centre of the ancient Greek world.

For Truthfulness

49. Almighty God, who hast sent the spirit of truth... (Bishop Westcott)

See 44.

Pericles

For Guidance

50. O God, foreasmuch without thee... (Book of Common Prayer)

See 14.

52. O Lord, give us more charity... (Henry Alford)

See 34.

54. Give us a sense of humour, Lord... (Thomas Webb)

Thomas Henry Basil Webb was the only son of Lieut-Colonel Sir Henry Webb. Born in 1898, he was educated at Winchester College. Sadly, he was killed on the Somme on 1st December 1917, aged 19. He wrote these words at the age of 12; he was also the author of the Chester Cathedral Refectory prayer, which remains in use today.

For our country
56. Lord, bless this kingdom... (William Laud)
William Laud (1573-1645) was Archbishop of Canterbury from 1633 to 1645. One of the High Church Caroline divines, he opposed radical forms of Puritanism. This, and his support for King Charles I, resulted in his beheading in the midst of the English Civil War.

For the Queen
57. Almighty God, fountain of all goodness... (Prayer Book 1928, modified)
The 1928 Prayer Book was approved in 1927 by the Church Assembly of the Church of England. However, its authorization was defeated in the House of Commons the following year. In 1966, with some changes, it was authorized as legal for public worship, as the First Series of Alternative Services. *Subsequently it made up much of the* Alternative Service Book *and its successor,* Common Worship.

58. Eternal God, who rulest in the kingdoms of men... (Jeremy Taylor)
Son (1613-1667) of a barber who became chaplain to King Charles I and was imprisoned several times after the Parliamentary victory in the Civil Wars. He spent several years writing, studying and teaching in Wales and Ireland, and at the Restoration was appointed Bishop of Down and Connor, and also vice-chancellor of Dublin University.

The Scouts
61. Give us, O Lord, a steadfast heart... (St Thomas Aquinas)
Thomas Aquinas (1225-1274) was an Italian Dominican priest of the Roman Catholic Church, and an immensely influential philosopher and theologian. Thomas is held in the Catholic Church to be the model teacher for those studying for the priesthood. He is considered the Church's greatest theologian and philosopher.

St Thomas Aquinas

For Help in Learning

62. O Lord Jesus Christ, eternal wisdom of the Father… (John Hampden)

The statesman and patriot John Hampden (1594-1643) came from a prominent Buckinghamshire family who were Lords of Great and Little Hampden. Little is known of his early life although it is believed that at the age of six he was sent to the free Grammar School at Thame. For many, Hampden is seen as the central figure at the start of the English Revolution, and it is his statue that was selected by the Victorians as a symbol to take its place at the entrance to the Central Lobby in Palace of Westminster.

63. O Lord our God, grant us grace… (St Anselm)

St Anselm

Anselm of Canterbury (1033-1109) was a Benedictine monk, a philosopher, and a prelate of the Church who held the office of Archbishop of Canterbury from 1093 to 1109. Called the founder of scholasticism, he is famous as the originator of the famous 'ontological argument' for the existence of God. He was canonized in 1494.

65. May the strength of God pilot us… (St Patrick)

Patron saint of Ireland. As a boy, he was captured by pirates while working as a herdsman in Wales during the Fifth Century, and carried off to Ireland as a slave. After escaping several years later, he said that he had a vision calling him back to preach there. He baptised thousands of people, including members of several royal families, and is said to be buried in Down Cathedral.

66. O most merciful Redeemer… (St Richard)

Richard of Chichester (also known as Richard de Wych or variations thereof) (1197 -1253) is a saint (canonized 1262) who was Bishop of Chichester. His shrine in Chichester Cathedral was a richly-decorated centre of pilgrimage which was destroyed in 1538. The modern St Richard's Shrine, re-established in 1930, is located in the retro-quire of Chichester Cathedral.

67. O Lord Jesus Christ, who art the Way... (Erasmus)

Leading Renaissance humanist, Catholic priest and theologian (c1466-1536) who was responsible for influential new Latin and Greek editions of the New Testament in the early 16th Century. Although he was committed to reforming the Church from within, he refused to support Martin Luther's Reformist movement, and remained a loyal Roman Catholic. His writings included the satirical In Praise of Folly, Handbook of a Christian Knight *and* Education of a Christian Prince, *written for the future Holy Roman Emperor, Charles V.*

Erasmus

68. Grant to us, O Lord...
(Thomas à Kempis)

Fifteenth century Catholic monk and copyist (1380-1471), author of The Imitation of Christ, *a handbook for the spiritual life. He was born at Kempen, in the diocese of Cologne, but was educated at Deventer, in the Netherlands and spent most of his life in the Monastery of Mount St Agnes, near Zwolle.*

69. Lord, make us instruments of thy peace... (St Francis)

Saint Francis of Assisi (1181-1226). The son of a prosperous merchant in the central Italian town of Assisi, Francis became an ascetic and a beggar after a vision during a serious illness. Apart from the famous Franciscan Order of monks, he founded the Order of St. Clare for nuns, known as the Poor Clares, and also the Third Order of St Francis for the lay community. He was canonised in 1228, shortly after his death.

For the Peace of the World

75. Almighty God, from whom all thoughts of truth and peace proceed...
(Bishop Paget)

The son of a surgeon, the Rt Rev Francis Paget (1851-1911) was Regius Professor of Pastoral Theology at Oxford University and Dean of Christ Church College. He was ordained Bishop of Oxford in 1901 and served until his death ten years later, being known not just for his distinction as a scholar but also as an active campaigner for the needy.

76. Almighty God and most merciful Father... (Armistice Day)

This was adapted from the Armistice Day ceremony of 1931. Nowadays known as Remembrance Day (11th November), it has been observed since the end of World War I to remember the members of their armed forces who have died in the line of duty.

For All Men

77. O God, the creator and preserver... (Bishop Gunning)

Royalist cleric (1614-1684) under King Charles I who was known for his eloquent preaching. He lived quietly under the Commonwealth following King Charles's execution but returned to favour with the Restoration, being appointed to positions in Canterbury Cathedral and Cambridge University. In 1669 he was consecrated Bishop of Chichester, and five years later, Bishop of Ely.

The Commons' Prayer

84. Almighty God, by whom alone Kings reign... ('17th century or earlier')

Although little known outside the Palace of Westminster, this prayer (c1661) was said daily by the Speaker's Chaplain before every sitting of the House of Commons from 1661 until 1997. It was then replaced (to the regret of some MPs) by a shorter and more modern version.

Evening

85. O God, from whom all holy desires... (Book of Common Prayer)

See 14.

86. Lighten our darkness... (Book of Common Prayer)

See 14.

88. Save us, O Lord, waking... (Breviarium Romanum)

The volume containing the daily hours of Roman Catholic prayer was published as the Breviarium Romanum (Roman Breviary) until the reforms of Paul VI, when it became known as the Liturgy of the Hours.

89. Keep us, Lord, so awake in the duties of our calling... (John Donne) *English poet, satirist and priest (c1572-1631). Although brought up as a Catholic, Donne was ordained as a Church of England minister after his works attracted the attention of King James I, and became a Royal Chaplain in 1615. Six years later, he was appointed Dean of St Pauls. His prayers and meditations were published under the title Devotions upon Emergent Occasions, and he was well known for his tightly argued but highly emotional sermons. As a writer of epigrams, songs, elegies and satires, he is considered to be the most important of the Metaphysical Poets of the 17th Century.*

John Donne

Closing Prayers

96. The grace of our Lord Jesus Christ...

This familiar Grace Prayer is based on Paul's prayer at the end of 2 Corinthians 13.

SUBSCRIBERS

Neil Anderson, South Australia

Richard Armitage, Cheltenham

Michael N Atkinson, Ulverston

Paul Balderstone, Almondbury

Prof Colin Bamford, Dalton

Tom Berry, Knowl Hill

Lucy Berry, Knowl Hill

Bob Brook, Marsh

Norman Burluraux, Germany

David A Bush, Porthcawl

Geoffrey R Butters, Fixby

Reggie Byram, Birkby

Trevor T Carter, Almondbury

James Clayton, Norwich

Graham Cliffe, Almondbury

Keith Crawshaw, Almondbury

Roger Dowling, Lymm

John Dyson, Norway

John Eastwood, Sowerby Bridge

Haydn Foster, Ossett

Chris Graley, Farnley Tyas

Terry Green, Chester

Andrew Haigh, Almondbury

Dr John A Hargreaves, Halifax

Richard G Hey, Fenay Bridge

Ian Hinchliff, Honley

Gerald Hinchliffe, Wollaton

Andrew K Hirst, Henley-in-Arden

Marion Holmes, Almondbury

Bryan Hopkinson, Huddersfield

Bernard Hoyle, Newsome

King James's School, Almondbury

Robert Lamb, Oldham

Ken Leech, Australia

Barry Livesey, Clifton

Christopher Mann, Whitwell

David Matthews, Bognor Regis

Mark Merrill, Salisbury

Sophie Moodie, Argyll and Bute

David Morphet, London

Robert Partridge, Sheffield

David Pedley, Honley

Hilary and Brian Pollard, Huddersfield

Walter Raleigh, Lindley

Alison Roberts, Herne Hill

Christopher Roberts, Hampstead

Penny Roberts, Brixton

Stuart W Roebuck, Newsome

Dr Edward Royle, York

Sargeant family, Ossett,

Rev J P Senior, Almondbury

E Selwyn Shaw, Almondbury

Ian Smallwood, Nottingham

Alan D Smith, Brough

Gerald Stead, Lindley

Abi Taylor, Knowl Hill

Andrew Taylor, Knowl Hill

Beccy Taylor, Knowl Hill

Denis Taylor, Halifax

Edward J Taylor, Birkby

J Richard Taylor, Ossett

J D Taylor, Almondbury

Jack Taylor, Halifax

Marcus J Taylor, Singapore

Sam Taylor, Knowl Hill

Simon J Taylor, Ossett

Timothy R Taylor, Honley

Timlin family, Ossett,

Ross and Jan Trembath, Sydney

Dr J P Toomey, Stourport-on-Severn

Ann Walker, Otley

Peter Warry, York

Mike Wilkinson, Telford

Anthony Withers, Derby

The Woolpack, Almondbury